Jacob Ebersoll

THE IMMIGRANT OF
1763
AND
HIS DESCENDANTS

Robert A. Heilman

HERITAGE BOOKS
2008

HERITAGE BOOKS

AN IMPRINT OF HERITAGE BOOKS, INC.

Books, CDs, and more—Worldwide

For our listing of thousands of titles see our website
at
www.HeritageBooks.com

Published 2008 by
HERITAGE BOOKS, INC.
Publishing Division
100 Railroad Ave. #104
Westminster, Maryland 21157

International Standard Book Numbers
Paperbound: 978-0-7884-3740-3
Clothbound: 978-0-7884-7671-6

Preface

During the eighteenth century, six men with the surname *Ebersole* emigrated from Bern, Switzerland, to the (at the time) Province of Pennsylvania.

Provincial records exist for Abraham Ebersole, who arrived in 1727; as well as for Yost, Johannes and Peter Ebersole, who arrived in 1739. Johannes and Peter were sons of Yost, a nickname for Joseph. Then came Carl; and finally, Jacob, who arrived in 1763 and settled in Donegal Township, Lancaster County.

A few "old Ebersole family papers," given to me by my mother, indicated that Jacob Ebersole, the immigrant of 1763, was clearly my maternal ancestor. Thus began the search for Jabob Ebersole's many descendants and the compilation of the record of *Jacob Ebersoll, the Immigrant of 1763 and His Descendants*.

I used the register form, sometimes known as the "New England register form," in setting down this Ebersole genealogy on paper. Small case Roman numerals are used to indicate the order of birth. Arabic numerals are used to indicate those whose line is carried on by marriage and issue.

The string of names in brackets following each head of a family, each with a superscript type of number, shows the line of descent from the original family head through the successive generations. The superscript number indicates the generation.

I have made an effort to keep abbreviations to a minimum. Those most frequently used are as follows:

> b. = birth, born
> b. = burial, buried
> d. = death, died
> m. = marriage, married

In searching for information about the Ebersoles, I found a great variation in the spelling of the name Ebersole. Ebersole seems to be the most common or preferred spelling of the name. I also found Aebersohl, Ebersohl, Ebersol, Ebersoll and Eversole, along with a number of less common variations.

I have tried diligently to avoid errors. However, should there be any errors, I, alone, am to blame.

Acknowledgements

I am indebted to many people for the help I received from each and every one in putting this Ebersole genealogy together.

I must recognize David Bachman, a knowledgeable and helpful volunteer at the Lebanon County Historical Society; as well as the Society's librarian, Christine Mason. Others who helped were Patricia Hillman, Evelyn Barnhard, Kenneth Long, Kathy Lewis of the Hershey-Derry Township Historical Society; and especially, Judy Eitner, the archivist for the county of Lancaster, Pennsylvania. John Gordon's family history, *The Family of Jacob and Kate Ebersole*, was immensely helpful.

To each of these persons, I owe a debt of gratitude. If I missed anyone who gave me assistance with this project, I beg their forgiveness.

JACOB EBERSOLL
THE IMMIGRANT OF 1763
AND
HIS DESCENDANTS

A Family History
Researched and Written
by
Robert A. Heilman

1. 130.JACOB EBERSOLL, the progenitor of this family of Ebersoles, emigrated form Bern Switzerland in the year 1763. He sailed form Rotterdam, Holland and last from Cowes, England aboard the ship, *Chance,* commanded by Captain Charles Smith. He arrived at Philadelphia in the Province of Pennsylvania on November 1, 1763.

Jacob traveled inland from Philadelphia to Donegal Township in Lancaster County where he settled. He died there in 1785.

All that is known about Jacob's wife is that her given name was Frances (Veronica).

Jacob's descendants changed the spelling of the surname from Ebeersoll to Ebersole. Other variations of the name are Ebersohl, Ebersol.

Issue:

2.	i. John
3.	ii. Jacob
4.	iii. Christian who married Magdalena
5.	iv. Martin
6.	v. Daniel

References:
Gerberich, Albert H., *The Ebersoles of Early Lancaster County*, Mennonite
    Research Journal, Vol. 4, No. 1, pp. 1,2
Lancaster County, Pa. Deeds, Book S, Vol. 3, pp. 206, 207, 208, 209, 210,
    211
Ibid., Vol. 13, p. 103
Lancaster County Wills, Will of Jacob Ebersole, Book

2. JOHN EBERSOLE [Jacob[1]], son of Jacob and Frances Ebersole was born in Donegal Township, Lancaster County, Pa. His date of birth is not now known. His death occurred sometime in 1814.

John was married to Elizabeth Bossler of whom we know nothing.

Presumably John Ebersole was a farmer.

Issue:

7.   i. Mathias B.
          ii. Barbara B. who married John Hoffman
8.   iii. Jacob B., b. February 1785
          iv. Annie B. who married Jacob Hoffman
          v. Daniel B.
          vi. John B. who married Mary Weaver

References:

Gerberich, Albert H., *The Ebersoles of Early Lancaster County,* Mennonite
      Research Journal, Vol. 4, No. 1, pp. 1,2
Lancaster County, Pa. Deeds, Book S, Vol. 3, pp. 206, 207, 208, 209, 210,
      211
Lancaster County, Pa. Orphans Court Records, Miscellaneous Book
      1813 - 1816, p. 200
Ibid., Petition for appointment of guardian for Daniel Ebersole
Dauphin County, Pa. Wills, Will of Mathias Blasser

3. JACOB EBERSOLE [Jacob[1]], son of Jacob and Frances Ebersole
was born in Donegal Township, Lancaster County, Pa. about 1757. He died
February 21, 1828 in Donegal Township, Lancaster County, Pa.

Jacob was married to Veronica Mellinger, daughter of Benedict and Mary
(Hershey) Mellinger. Veronica died circa 1822.

Jacob was probably a farmer and a deacon in the Mennonite Church.

Issue:

9.   i. David Mellinger, b. February 27, 1786
          ii. Mary who married Christian Stoner
10.   iii. Jacob M., b. August 30, 1787
          iv. Fanny, b. 1791 who married Jacob Ebersole
          v. Veronica, b. 1795 Veronica married Isaac Etter.

References:

Gerberich, Albert H., *The Ebersoles of Lancaster County,* Mennonite
Research
      Journal, Vol. 4, No. 1, pp. 1, 2
Lancaster County, Pa. Deeds, Vol. 11, p. 73
Ibid., Vol. 13, pp. 101, 103

"   Book Y, Vol. 7, p. 497
"   Book Y, Vol. 8, p. 290
Lancaster County, Pa. Wills, Will of Jacob Ebersole, Sen., Book P, Vol. 1,
        p. 156
Ibid., Will of Benedict Mellinger, Will Book , Vol. 1, p. 397

4. CHRISTIAN EBERSOLE [Jacob[1]], son of Jacob and Frances
Ebersole was born in Donegal Township, Lancaster County, Pa. Neither his
date of birth or his date of death are now known.

   Christian Ebersole married three times; first to Magdalena Gensinger,
second to Barbara Rutt, daughter of Peter Rutt and third to Annie Weber
(Weaver), daughter of John Weber. Annie was born about 1760 and died in
1842.

   Christian Ebersole was most likely a farmer.

   Issue:

	i.	Fannie G. who married John Ebersole
11.	ii.	Jacob G., b. 1786/87
	iii.	Magdalena G., b. November 1789; d. 1864. Magddalena married Christian Rutt, b. September 28, 1789; d, March 14,1850. Both are buried in the Rutt graveyard south of Elizabethtown, Pa.
12.	iv.	Peter R., b. December 6, 1790
13.	v.	John R., b. May 2, 1793
14.	vi.	Christian R., b. February 19, 1794
	vii.	Anna R. who married Christian Mellinger
15.	viii.	Henry R., b. August 24, 1797
16,	ix.	Samuel W., b. February 14, 1802

   References:

Gerberich, Albert H., *The Ebersoles of Early Lancaster County*, Mennonite
        Research Journal, Vol.4, No. 1, pp. 1, 2
Lancaster County, Pa. Deeds, Book DD, Vol. 2, p. 361
Lancaster County Orphans Court Records, Miscellaneous Book 1806-1808,
        p. 241
Lancaster County, Pa. Wills, Will of Peter Rutt, Will Book I, Vol. 1, p.390
Lancaster Mennonite Historical Society Abstracts and Index of Orphans Court
        of Lancaster County, 1740 - 1804

5. MARTIN Ebersole [Jacob[1]], son of Jacob and Frances Ebersole, was born in Lancaster County, Pa., probably in Donegal Township. Nothing is now known of his birth or death.

Martin Ebersole married Barbara Gensinger, the daughter of Daniel Gensinger.

Issue:

17.	i. John, b. February 15, 1786
18.	ii. Barbara, b. 1792
	iii. Martha
	iv. David
19.	v. Jacob, b. June 30, 1795

References:

Heads of Families, First Census of the U. S.: 1790, Pennsylvania, Maytown, Lancaster County, p. 142

Lancaster Mennonite Historical Society *Abstract and Index Orphans' Court Records of Lancaster County, 740 - 1804,*

Kauffman, Charles F., *A Genealogy and History of the Kauffman - Coffman Families of North America*, p. 62

Lancaster County, Pa. Deeds, Book DD, Vol. 2, p. 361

Lancaster County Orphans Court Records, Bond Book W, Vol. 1, p. 444

Mennonite Research Journal, Vol. III, No. 3, p. 36

Wenger, Samuel S., *The Wenger Book: A Foundation Book of American Wengers,* p. 1074

6. DANIEL EBERSOLE [Jacob[1]], son of Jacob and Frances Ebersole was born December 26, 1768 in Lancaster County, Pa., probably in Donegal Township where he died about the year 1799.

On April 5, 1791 Daniel married Anna Daumler.

Issue: (all born in Lancaster County, Pa.)

    i. Jacob
    ii. John
    iii. Elizabeth
    iv. Anna

        Both Anna and Elizabeth were baptized December 22, 1809.

References:

Early Marriage Records, 1731 - 1850, inclusive, of the Trinity Lutheran Church, Lancaster, Pa.

Gerberich, Albert H., *The Ebersoles of Early Lancaster County,* Mennonite Research Journal, Vol. 4, No. 1, pp. 1, 2

Lancaster County, Pa. Deeds, Book E, Vol. 3, p. 513
Lancaster County Orphans Court Records, Miscellaneous Book 1796 - 1801,
    p. 342
Ibid., Miscellaneous Book, 1806 - 1808, p. 273
Letters of Administration granted to the Executors of the estate of Daniel
    Ebersole by the Registrar for the Probate of Wills, July 3, 1799.

7. MATHIAS B. EBERSOLE [John[2], Jacob[1]], son of John and
Elizabeth (Bossler) Ebersole was born in Lancaster County, Pa., probably in
Donegal Township. The dates of his birth and death are not now known.
   On January 19, 1808 Mathias married Catharine Foltz (Folz on the church
marriage record) at Lancaster, Pa.
        Issue:
                i. John, b. 1813; d. unmarried June 11, 1884 at
                    Harrisonburg, Va. John was a presbyterian.
                ii. Mathias Jr., b. 1828
        References:
*Early Marriage Records, 1731 to 1850, inclusive, of the Trinity Lutheran
    Church, Lancaster, Pa.*, Book No. 4, p. 65, Donegal Chapter, DAR,
    Lancaster, Pa., 1950
Gerberich, Albert H., *The Ebersoles of Early Lancaster County,* Mennonite
    Research Journal, Vol. 4, No. 1 pp. 1,2
Herald of Truth, July 15, 1884, p. 221
U. S. Census, 1850, Pennsylvania, Dauphin County, Swatara Township, p.
196

8. JACOB BOSSLER EBERSOLE [John[2], Jacob[1]], son of John and
Elizabeth (Bossler) Ebersole was born in February 1785 in Lancaster County,
Pa., probably in Donegal Township. He died in October of 1843 and is
buried at Stauffer's Mennonite Church Cemetery, Bachmanville, Dauphin
County, Pa. Unfortunately, his gravestone is weathered to the point that the
days of the month are not legible.
   Family papers show that Jacob married Elizabeth Moyer on January 16,
1807. Records of the Trinity Lutheran Church, Lancaster, Pa. give the date
of marriage as January 19, 1808.
   Jacob was a farmer near Campbelltown, Lebanon County, Pa. He and his
family were Mennonites.
        Issue:

20.	i. Leah
	ii. Barbara Moyer who married Solomon Weir.
21	iii. John Moyer, b. June 26, 1811
22	iv. Jacob Moyer, b. July 15, 1815
23	v. Daniel Moyer, b. February 28, 1817

References:

Early Marriage Records, 1731 to 1850, inclusive, of the Trinity   Lutheran Church, Lancaster, Pa., Book No. 4, p. 65, Donegal
 Chapter of the DAR, Lancaster, Pa.
Ebersole family papers currently in the author's possession
Inscriptions, Stauffer's Mennonite Church Cemetery, Bachmanville,
 Dauphin County, Pa.
Middletown Journal, Middletown, Pa., March 15, 1895

9. DAVID MELLINGER EBERSOLE [Jacob[2], Jacob[1]], son of Jacob and Veronica (Mellinger) Ebersole was born February 27, 1786 in Lancaster County, Pa., probably in Donegal Township. He died February 14, 1861 and is buried in the Ebersole family cemetery in Conoy Township, Lancaster County, Pa.

David was married twice. His first wife was Gertrude Nissley, daughter of John Nissley. Gertrude was born September 21, 1780 and died January 10, 1821. She, too, is buried in the Ebersole family cemetery with her husband.
 Issue:

	i. Maria N., (Fannie N.), b. February 7, 1809. Fannie married Henry B. Ebersole.(See #15, Henry B. Ebersole.)
24	ii. John David, b. January 10, 1811
	iii. Jacob, b. January 29, 1813

After the death of his first wife, David married a second time to Esther Burkholder Lehman, a widow, on August 12, 1821. Esther was born August 24, 1798 and died July 12, 1879. She is buried in the Ebersole family cemetery, near Bainbridge, Pa.
 Issue:

25	iv. Abraham B., b. September 8, 1822
26	v. Elisabeth B., b. December 26, 1824
27	vi. Mary B., b. 1827
28	vii. Samuel D., b. October 21, 1829
29	viii. David B., b. circa 1832
	ix. Barbara B., b. circa 1839. Barbara married Jacob Witmer

References:

Birth Record from David M. Ebersole family Bible, Lancaster Mennonite
    Historical   Society, Lancaster, Pa.
Burkholder Reunion Booklet, 1928, p. 33
Ellis & Evans, *History of Lancaster County, Pennsylvania*, p. 340
Herald of Truth, August 1879, p. 157
Mennonite Research Journal, Vol. VII, No. 1, p. 41
Ibid., Vol. V, No. 3
Lancaster County, Pa. Deeds, Book Q, Vol. 7, p. 60
Ibid., Book 13, p. 103
  "   Book B, Vol. 9, p. 531
Lancaster County, Pa. Orphans Court Records, Accounts and Reports
    Book 15, p. 329
Lancaster County, Pa. Wills, Will of David M. Ebersole, Will Book   X,
    Vol. 1, p. 206
Ibid., Will of John Nissley, Will Book M, Vol. 1, p. 330
Retherford, Audrey L., *Cemetery Records of Conoy Township*
U. S. Census, 1850, Pennsylvania, Lancaster County, Conoy Township, p.
301
Weaver, Martin G., *Mennonites of the Lancaster Conference*

10. JACOB M. EBERSOLE [Jacob[2], Jacob[1]], son of Jacob and
Veronica (Mellinger) Ebersole was born August 30, 1787 in Lancaster
County, probably in Donegal Township. He died September 24, 1873 and is
buried on the Risser farm cemetery.

March 29, 1814, Jacob M. Ebersole married Barbara Kauffman. She was
born October 27, 1792 and died September 27, 1858. Barbara is buried on
the Risser farm with her husband.

Issue:

    i. Fannie K., b. February 10, 1815; d. April 12, 1836. Bur.
Risser farm cemetery.

    ii. Michael K., b. January 15, 1817; d. October 29, 1876.
Bur. Risser farm.

    iii. Elizabeth K., b. November 15, 1818; d. Mary 15, 1905.
Bur. Risser Farm. Elizabeth married John Landis, b. 1815;
d. May   9, 1877.

    iv. David K., b. December 24, 1820; d. July 24, 1822Bur.
Risser farm.

30..   v. Christian K., b. April 13, 1823
             vi. Jacob K., b. January 1826; d. August 14, 1874
             vii. Daniel K., b. May 23, 1828; d. June 29, 1846.
                  Bur. Risser farm.
31.   viii. Henry K., b. November 5, 1830
             ix. Barbara K., b. April 26, 1833; d. March 7, 1857.
                  Bur. Risser farm. (Audrey Retherford says she died
                  March 6.)
             x. Anna K., b. August 21, 1837; d. February 27, 1923.
      References:
Herald of Truth, September 1874, p. 159
Lancaster County Deeds, Book Y, Vol. 8, pp. 287, 288, 290
Ibid., Book Y, Vol. 7, p. 499
Kauffman Genealogy, p. 43
Retherford, Audrey, *Cemetery Records*, p. 10

11. JACOB G. EBERSOLE [Christian[2], Jacob[1]], son of Christian and
Magdalena (Gensinger) Ebersole was born circa 1787 in Lancaster County,
Pa., probably in Donegal Township. He died April 5, 1861 in Conoy
Township, Lancaster County, Pa.
      Jacob G. Ebersole married Barbara _____ on March 19, 1814. His second
wife was Anna Rutt.
      Issue:
32.   i. Joseph, b. December 4, 1809
             ii. Barbara, b. February 16, 1813. Barbara married Joseph
                  Good.
33.   iii. Christian, b. February 24, 1815
             iv. Anna, b. February 1, 1817. Anna married Henry Brenneman
             v, Veronica, b. June 11, 1819
             vi. Peter R., b. January 14, 1821; d. May 1, 1853. Bur.
                  Ebersole Cemetery, near Bainbridge.
34.   vii. Solomon R., b. November 15, 1822
35.   viii. John R., b. May 26, 1826
             ix. Maria, b. June 18, 1838
      References:
Lancaster County, Pa. Wills, Will of Jacob G. Ebersole, Will Book X,
      Vol. 1, p. 230
Lancaster County, Pa. Deeds, Book A, Vol. 9, p. 597

Ibid., Book Y, Vol. 7, p. 497
   "   Book O, Vol. 12, p. 17
Lancaster County Orphans Court Records, Misc. Book 1859 - 1861,
      p. 618
Mennonite Research Journal, Vol. 3, No. 3, p. 36
Ibid., Vol. 4, No. 1, pp. 1, 2
Kauffman, Charles F., *A Genealogy and History of the Kauffman - Coffman
Families of North America*, p.
Ebersole family Bible
Retherford, Audrey, *Cemetery Records of Conoy Township*
Weaver, Martin G., *Mennonites of Lancaster Conference*, p. 212

12. PETER R. EBERSOLE [Christian[2], Jacob[1]] son of Christian and Barbara (Rutt) Ebersole was born December 6, 1790 in Lancaster County, Pa., probably in Donegal Township. He died December 12, 1870 and is buried in the Ebersole family cemetery, about 1/2 mile west of Good's Meeting House in Conoy Township, Lancaster County, Pa.

Peter R. Ebersole married Mary Risser who was born January 15, 1793. (*The Herald of Truth* says Mary was born February 15, 1793,) She died April 20, 1866 and is buried with her husband in the Ebersole family cemetery, near Good's Meeting House.

Peter R. Ebersole was a Mennonite Bishop.

Issue:

	i.	Barbara R., b. December 21, 1820; d. unmarried July 3, 1906. Bur. in Ebersole family cemetery, 1/2 mile west of Good's Meeting House.
36.	ii.	Peter R., b. April 2, 1822
	iii.	Anna R., b. January 16, 1831; d. September 29, 1897. Anna married Jacob Ebersole ?
	iv.	Veronica R. (Fannie R.), b. July 11, 1829; d. June 15, 1892. Veronica married John E. Ebersole.
37.	v.	Jacob R. Ebersole, b. February 22, 1834
	vi.	Mary R., b. November 23, 1825; d. April 30, 1893. Mary was married to Christian Ebersole (See # 15).???

References:

Beers, J. H. Co., *Biographical Annals of Lancaster County, Pa.* 1903,
      p. 861
Gerberich, Albert H., Gerberich Collection of Gravestone Inscriptions,

Lancaster County, Ebersole Burying Ground, p. 202
Herald of Truth, May 1866, p. 44
Ibid., July 1, 1893, p. 215
Inscriptions, Ebersole family cemetery, west of Good's Meeting   House,
Conoy Township, Lancaster County, Pa.
Inscriptions, Good's Mennonite Cemetery, south of Elizabethtown,   Pa.
Lancaster County, Pa. Wills, Will of Peter R. Ebersole, Will Book   A,
    Vol. 2, p. 137
Mennonite Research Journal, Vol. 5, No. 1, p. 2
Retherford, Audrey, *Cemetery Records, etc.*
U. S. Census, 1850, Pennsylvania, Lancaster County, Conoy Township, p.
300
Weaver, Martin G., *Mennonites of Lancaster Conference, p. 99*

13. JOHN R. EBERSOLE [Christian[2], Jacob[1]], son of Christian and Barbara (Rutt) Ebersole was born May 2, 1793 in Lancaster County, Pa., probably in Donegal Township. He died April 18, 1846 in Conoy Township, Lancaster County and is buried in the Mt. Tunnel Cemetery, Elizabethtown, Pa.

John R. Ebersole was married three times. His first wife was Annie Eshelman who was born May 16, 1796 and who died August 16, 1821. His second wife was Sarah Ann Gilbert and his third wife was Sarah Souders. Sarah Souders was born January 29, 1811 and died January 13, 1896. She is buried at Mt. Tunnel with her husband.

Issue:
   i. Catharine who married John L. Good
   ii. John L., b. May 6, 1835; d. February 10, 1890. John
       married Fannie ____, b. 1836; d. January 12, 1917.
       Both are buried in the Mt. Tunnel Cemetery,
       Elizabethtown, Pa.
   iii. Levi S., b. 1838
   iv. Fanny, b. March 3, 1840. Fanny married November 14,
       1872 to John B. Engle.
   v. Aaron S., b. April 12, 1844; d. March 8, 1918. Bur.
       Mt. Tunnel Cemetery.
   vi. Sarah Ann who married John F. Balmer on November
       18, 1866.
   vii. Abraham d. unmarried December 20, 1853 ?

viii. Elisabeth

ix. Christian

References:

Engle, Morris M., *History of the Engle Family in America 1754 - 1927,*
    p. 127
Genealogical Card Catalog, Lancaster Mennonite Historical Society,
Lancaster, Pa.
Herald of Truth, March 1, 1896
Ibid., June 1, 1896, p. 174
Inscriptions, Mt. Tunnel Cemetery, Elizabethtown, Pa.
Lancaster County, Pa. Orphans Court Records, Miscellaneous Book
    1844 - 1847, p. 462
Ibid., Miscellaneous Book 1847 - 1848, pp. 281, 471
Lancaster County, Pa. Wills, Will of John Ebersole, Will Book U, Vol. 1, p.
106
Ibid., Will of Sarah Ann Ebersole, Will Book L, Vol. 2, p. 414
Lancaster County, Pa. Deeds, Book K, Vol. 7, p. 191
Ibid., Book U, Vol. 8, p. 602
Retherford, Audrey L., *Cemetery Records, etc.*

14. CHRISTIAN R. EBERSOLE [Christian[2], Jacob[1]], son of Christian
and Barbara (Rutt) Ebersole was born February 19, 1794 in Lancaster
County, Pa., probably in Donegal Township. He died September 10, 1865.

Christian married twice. His first wife was Anna Frey. Anna was born
August 28, 1789 and died December 25, 1838. His second wife was Mary
Brubaker. She was born October 3, 1812 and died May 26, 1889.

Issue:

38.   i. John Frey, b. March 16, 1829
            ii. Fannie
           iii. Jacob
            iv. Anna
             v. Elizabeth Frey, b. November 15, 1815; d. March 28,
                1908 in Letterkenny Township, Franklin County, Pa.
                Bur. Frey family cemetery.
            vi. Daniel
           vii. Christian

References:

Gospel Herald, May 2, 1908, p. 79

15. HENRY RUTT EBERSOLE [Chrisitian², Jacob¹], son of Christian and Barbara (Rutt) Ebersole was born August 24, 1797 in Lancaster County, Pa., probably in Donegal Township. He died October 14, 1842 in Conoy Township, Lancaster County and is buried in the Ebersole Cemetery near Bainbridge, Pa.

Henry married Fannie N. Ebersole, the daughter of David M. and Gertrude (Nissley) Ebersole. Fannie was born February 7, 1809 and died February 26, 1858. She is buried with her husband in the Ebersole family cemetery, near Bainbridge. (See # 9, p. 4)???

Issue:

    i. Christian E., b. September 28, 1826; d. December 31, 1857. Bur. Ebersole cemetery.

    ii. Henry E., b. March 17, 1829; d. November 28, 1860. Bur. Ebersole cemetery.

    iii. David, b. February 6, 1825; d. April 25, 1836. Bur. Ebersole cemetery.

    iv. Ann, b. January 27, 1840. Ann married Christian Martin Gish, b. September 6, 1827; d. February 12, 1903.

    v. Moses E., b. February 27, 1837; d. February 15, 1846. Bur. Ebersole cemetery.

References:
Lancaster County Orphans Court Records, Bond Book R, Vol. 1, p. 215
Ibid., Miscellaneous Book 1845 - 1850, p. 110
Retherford, Audrey L., *Cemetery Records, etc.*

16. SAMUEL W. EBERSOLE [Christian², Jacob¹], son of Christian and Annie (Weber) Ebersole was born February 14, 1802 in Lancaster County, Pa. He died October 30, 1879.

Samuel was married to Sarah Shenk who was born April 22, 1808. She died April 3, 1878. Both are buried in the Ebersole Cemetery.

Issue:

    i. Elizabeth, b. 1827; d. 1912. Elizabeth married Daniel Ebersole.

References:
Inscriptions, Ebersole family cemetery

17. JOHN EBERSOLE [Martin², Jacob¹], son of Martin and Barbara (Gensinger) Ebersole was born February 15, 1786 in Lancaster County, Pa., probably in Donegal Township. He died July 10, 1864 in Conoy Township.

John married Adaline Weaver who was born April 13, 1779 and who died October 2, 1858. She is buried in the Ebersole Cemetery, north of Bainbridge, Pa.

Issue:

39.   i. Susanna, b. April 10, 1810

           ii. Barbara who married John Moyer

         iii. Daniel

         iv. John

         v. George

40.   vi. Martin

References:

Lancaster County Deeds, Book L, Vol. 9, p. 184

Lancaster County Orphans Court Records, Bond Book L, Vol. 9, p. 293

Ibid., Miscellaneous Book 1863 - 1865, p. 299

Retherford, Audrey L., *Cemetery Records, etc.*

Wenger, Samuel S., *The Wenger Book: A Foundation Book of American Wengers*, p. 1103

18. BARBARA EBERSOLE [Martin^2, Jacob^1],daughter of Martin and Barbara (Gensinger) Ebersole was born in 1792 She died in 1820.

Barbara was married to John Stoner Kauffman who was born February 16, 1792. He died circa 1820.

    Issue:

        i. Barbara who married Samuel Burkholder and moved to Adams County, Pa. Samuel, son of Benjamin and Mary (Martin) Burkholder, was born June 8, 1793 at Florin (?), Lancaster County, Pa. He died January 27, 1840 and is buried at the Kraybill Mennonite Cemetery.

  References:

19. JACOB EBERSOLE [Martin^2, Jacob^1], son of Martin and Barbara (Gensinger) Ebersole was born June 30, 1795 in Lancaster County, Pa., probably in Donegal Township. He died in a "limb accident" December 12, 1867 in Lancaster County, Pa., probably in Conoy Township.

Jacob married Veronica (Fannie) Mellinger who was born August 24, 1791 and who died April 6, 1850. Jacob then married a second time to Barbara

Lehman Witmer, a widow, who was born November 29, 1797 and who died September 27, 1882. Barbara is buried in the cemetery at Stauffer's Mennonite Church Bachmanville, Dauphin County, Pa. Barbara was the widow of Jacob Witmer before her marriage to Jacob Ebersole.

     Issue:

41.   i. Daniel, b. May 6, 1821

     References:

Gordon, John, In liters

Herald of Truth, February 1868, p. 31

Inscriptions, Ebersole cemetery, Conoy Township, Lancaster County
     Historical Society, Lancaster, Pa.

Lancaster County, Pa. Wills, Will of Jacob Ebersole, Will Book Z,
     Vol. 1, p. 175

Lebanon County Historical Society, Lebanon, Pa., *Burials In Cemeteries*
     Mostly from Old Cemeteries on Farms

Retherford, Audrey L., *Cemetery Records of Conoy Township, etc.*,
     p. 6

20. LEAH EBERSOLE [Jacob B.[3], John[2], Jacob[1]], daughter of Jacob and Elizabeth (Moyer) Ebersole was born in Lancaster County, Pa. Neither her place of birth or date of birth are now known. She died at Oberlin, Pa. on a date not now known.

    On March 27, 1828 Leah Ebersole was married to Henry Light.

     Issue:

         i. Maria
         ii. Isaac
         iii. Barbara
         iv. Elizabeth m. John McCord

     References:

Middletown Journal, Middletown, Pa., March 15, 1895

Records of Zion Evangelical Lutheran Church, Hummelstown, Pa.

21. JOHN MOYER EBERSOLE [Jacob B.[3], John[2], Jacob[1]], son of Jacob B. and Elizabeth (Moyer) Ebersole was born June 26, 1811 in West Donegal Township, Lancaster County, Pa. He died July 11, 1887 and is buried in the churchyard of the Salem Reformed Church now UCC)), Campbelltown, Pa.

    On January 26, 1835, according to family records, John married Sarah H.

Arnold, of Manheim, Lancaster County, Pa. Sarah was the daughter of Peter Arnold and his wife, born Elizabeth Herchilroth. The records of Zion Lutheran Church, Harrisburg, Pa. show the date of marriage to be February 26, 1834. Sarah was born October 12, 1815 and died June 7, 1867. She is buried with her husband in the cemetery of the Salem Reformed Church, Campbelltown, Pa.

Although John M. and Sarah (Arnold) Ebersole were Mennonites, they and their daughters Sarah, Caroling and Anna were buried in a Reformed Church cemetery.

during the years that John M. Ebersole was a single man, he worked the family farm in the summer months and during the autumn and winter months he drove a six horse team to Philadelphia. He hauled wheat to Philadelphia and brought back merchandise. His team of horses pulled a very large wagon with a cloth top (most likely canvas) to protect his cargo. His wagon was quite likely very similar to the famous Conestoga wagon.

After his marriage to Sarah Arnold, he bought a farm along the road from Palmyra to Campbelltown and devoted the remainder of his life to farming.

Issue: (all born in Londonderry Twonship, Lebanon County, Pa.)

42. i. Daniel A., b. January 26, 1836
43. ii. Elizabeth A., b. July 1, 1837
44. iii. John A., b. December 2, 1838
45   iv. Elias A., b. March 19, 1840
     v. Sarah A., b. September 26, 1841; d. unmarried May 6, 1885 in Palmyra, Pa. Bur. Salem Reformed Church Cemetery, Campbelltown, Pa.
46. vi. Mary A., b. February 7, 1843
     vii. Anna A., b. February 11, 1845; d. unmarried May 27, 1923 in Palmyra, Pa. Bur. Salem Reformed Church Cemetery, Campbelltown, Pa.
     viii. Caroline, b. October 4, 1846; d. unmarried August 31, 1917. Bur. Salem Reformed Church Cemetery, Campbelltown, Pa.
     x. Leah, b. April 8, 1848; d. May 19, 1927. Bur. Mt. Annville Cemetery, Annville, Pa. Leah was married December 21, 1869 to Henry Fisher (also Fischer) who was born November 16, 1844. He died January 31, 1898 and is buried with his wife at the Mt.

Annville Cemetery. No issue. Leah's husband may have had the nickname "Harry." His niece Minerva Shenk, the daughter of Mary A. Ebersole Shenk, referred to him as "Uncle Harry," as did others.

47.   x. Jacob A., b. May 23, 1850

After the death of his wife, Sarah, John married a second time to Leah Grubb on September 2, 1870. Leah was born February 16, 1831. She died February 1, 1893 and is buried in the Salem Reformed Cemetery with others of her family.

References:

Annville Journal, Annville, Pa., January 5, 1917, April 18, 1908

Beers, J. H. Co., *Biographical Annals of Lebanon County,* p. 689

Early, J. W., *Palmyra Its History and Its Surroundings,* Publications of the Lebanon County Historical Society, Lebanon, Pa., Vol. IV, No. 9, p. 285

Ebersole family papers, now in the possession of Robert A. Heilman

Evening Report, Lebanon, Pa., January 26, 1916

Family Bible of Mary A. Ebersole, wife of Jacob Shenk

Francis, J. G., *Light Family of Lebanon County*, Vol. II, pp. 391, 399

Francis J. G., *History of the Kreider Family from the Pen of The   Rev. J. G. Francis,* Lebanon Daily News, Lebanon, Pa., June 26,   1919

Herald of Truth, July 1867, p. 112

Inscriptions, Salem Reformed Church Cemetery, Campbelltown, Pa.

Inscriptions, U. B. Cemetery, Annville, Lebanon County, Pa.

Lebanon County Independent, Lebanon, Pa., May 21, 1885

Parish Records of Zion Lutheran Church, Harrisburg, Pa.

The Lebanon Courier, Lebanon, Pa., June 20, 1867, May 20, 1885

Lebanon County, Pa. Wills, Will of John Ebersole, Book G, p. 132

Ibid., Will of Caroline Ebersole, Book K, p. 472

"   Will of Leah Ebersole, Book G, p. 768

"   Will of Annie A. Ebersole, Book L, p. 625

U. S. Census, 1850, Pennsylvania, Lebanon County, Londonderry Township, p. 306

22. JACOB MOYER EBERSOLE [Jacob B.[3], John[2], Jacob[1]], son of Jacob and Elizabeth (Moyer) Ebersole was born July 15, 1815 in West Donegal Township, Lancaster County, Pa. He died March 15, 1895 at

Middletown, Dauphin County, Pa. and is buried at the Swatara Hill Cemetery, near Middletown, Dauphin County, Pa..

Jacob was married to Barbara Gish December 4, 1845. Barbara was born February 1, 1811 and died March 13, 1851. She is buried on the Willis Hackman farm, 2 miles southeast of Elizabethtown, Lancaster County, Pa.

Issue:

48.   i. Elizabeth Gish, b. June 30, 1846
49.   II. Barbara Gish, b. November 27, 1847
50.   iii. John Gish, b. January 28, 1849

After the death of his wife Barbara, Jacob married a second time to Mary Moyer who was born February 20, 1835. She died March 8, 1915 and is buried in the churchyard of Risser's Mennonite Church, near Elizabethtown, Lancaster County, Pa.

           iv. Christian Moyer, b. May 4, 1852; d. June 9, 1862
51.   v. Jacob Moyer, b. July 1, 1854
           vi. Benjamin Moyer, b. October 9, 1856; d. May 27, 1862.
               Bur. Spring Creek Cemetery, Hershey, Pa.
           vii. Annie Moyer, b. August 2, 1859
           viii. Joseph Moyer, b. April 24, 1862; d. May 10, 1914.
               Bur. Risser's Mennonite Cemetery.
52.   ix. Samuel Moyer, b. April 28, 1864
53.   x. David Moyer, b. May 26, 1867
           x. Henry Moyer, b. September 22, 1869; d. July 29,
               1892. Bur. Swatara Hill Cemetery, east of Middletown,
               Pa.
           xi. Daniel Moyer, b. April 27, 1872; d. March 3, 1849.   Bur.
               Swatara Hill Cemetery, east of Middletown, Pa.

References:

Ebersole, Jacob, Family Bible, Bible Collection, Lebanon County
     Historical Society, Lebanon, Pa.
Evening Report, Lebanon, Pa., March 16, 1895
Gospel Herald, April 5, 1949, p. 333
Inscriptions, Bindnagel's Church Cemetery, Palmyra, Pa.
Inscriptions, Risser's Mennonite Cemetery, Elizabethtown, Pa.
Inscriptions, Swatara Hill Church of the Brethren Cemetery, east of
     Middletown, Dauphin County, Pa.
Lancaster County, Pa. Orphans Court Records, Bond Book O,
     Vol. 1, p. 251

Ibid., Account and Reports Book 4, p. 2
Lancaster County, Pa. Deeds, Book O, Vol. 12, p. 345
Lancaster County, Pa. Wills, Will of Daniel M. Ebersole, Book W,
    Vol. 3, p. 320
Middletown Journal, Middletown, Pa., March 15, 1895
Rineer, A. Hunter, *Lancaster County Cemeteries,* Vol. 24, Rissers
    Cemetery, Mt. Joy Township
Ibid., Vol. 24, Willis Hackman farm
U. S. Census, 1850, Pennsylvania, Lancaster County, Mt. Joy
    Township

23. DANIEL MOYER EBERSOLE [Jacob B.[3], John[2], Jacob[1]], son of
Jacob B. and Elizabeth (Moyer) Ebersole, was born February 28, 1817 in
East Donegal Township, Lancaster County, Pa. He died October 27, 1896 in
Chamberland County, Pa.

   Daniel was married to Lydia Keenports August 18, 1863. Lydia was born
May 13, 1838. She died January 25, 1902. She, too, is buried in
Chamberland County, Pa.

     Issue:

54.	i.	John B., b. October 4, 1863
	ii.	Annie C., b. December 13, 1866; d. February 19, 1953. Annie married Jacob M. Ebersole. (see #48)???
55.	iii.	Mary M., b. July 13, 1869

     References:

Records of Tabor Reformed Church, Lebanon, Pa.

24. JOHN DAVID EBERSOLE [David M.[3], Jacob[2], Jacob[1]], son of
David M. and his wife, Gertrude (Nissley] Ebersole, was born June 19, 1811
in Lancaster County, Pa. He died September 19, 1883 and is buried in
Good's Mennonite Cemetery, near Elizabethtown, Pa.

   John David Ebersole married Fanny B. Longenecker, the daughter of
Christian and Veronica (Brenneman) Longenecker on February 27, 1838.
Fanny was born November 22, 1812 and died November 29, 1888. She, too,
is buried at Good's Cemetery.

   John David Ebersole was a farmer and a Mennonite.

     Issue:

56	i.	Barbara L., b. March 12, 1839
57	ii.	Levi L., b. July 26, 1840

iii. Fanny, b. December 17, 1841. Fanny married Martin Rutt

58   iv. Anna, b. June 24, 1843

59   v. David L., b. August 14, 1844

vi. Christian, b. October 26, 1846; d. February 4, 1861.

vii. John, b. January 3, 1950; d. January 3, 1850

60   viii. Elizabeth (Lizzie), b. February 12, 1852

ix. Abraham L., b. December 20, 1853; d. January 10, 1861.

References:

Beers, J. H. & Co., *Biographical Annals of Lancaster County, Pa., 1903*, p. 1146

Gerberich, Albert H., *The Brenneman History*, p. 74

"   " *Collection of Gravestone Inscriptions, Good's Meeting House*, Microfilm Reel 2, Part 2, p. 187

Herald of Truth, December 15, 1888

History of Longacre - Longaker - Longenecker Family, pp. 126-128, 130--133, 135- 137

Inscriptions, Good's Mennonite Cemetery, near Elizabethtown, Pa.

Lancaster Examiner, Lancaster, Pa., March 3, 1838

U. S. Census, 1850, Pennsylvania, Lancaster County, West Donegal Township

25. ABRAHAM BURKHOLDER EBERSOLE [David M.³, Jacob², Jacob¹], son of David Mellinger and Esther (Burkholder) Lehman Ebersole was born in Lancaster County, Pa. on September 8, 1822. He died January 21. 1892 at Sterling, Illinois and is buried in the Science Ridge Cemetery, Sterling, Illinois.

On October 16, 1845 Abraham married Anna Ebersole Rutt.

Issue:

61   i. Elias Rutt, b. January 8, 1847

62   ii. Esther (Hettie), b. January 18, 1849

63   iii. Magdalena, b. March 9, 1851

64   iv. Anna R., b. July 26, 1853

65   v. Sabina, b. December 22, 1855

66   vi. Michael Rutt, b. June 15, 1858

vii. Abraham, b. May 1861; d. unmarried and is bur. in   the Mt. Olive Cemetery.

viii. Solomon R., b. August 1866; d. unmarried and is buried in the Science Ridge Cemetery, Sterling, Ill. 64.

67.   ix. Amos A., b. September 4, 1869

References:

Umble, John, *Descendants of Preacher Abraham Burkholder Ebersole and his Wife, Anna Ebersole Rutt*

U. S. Census, 1850, Pennsylvania, Lancaster County, Conoy Township, p. 301

26. ELIZABETH B. EBERSOLE [David M.[3], Jacob[2], Jacob[1]], daughter of David M. and Elizabeth (Burkholder) Lehman Ebersole was born December 26, 1824 in Conoy Township, Lancaster County, Pa. She died January 7, 1896 and is buried in Good's Mennonite Cemetery, near Elizabethtown, Pa.

On May 23, 1844 Elizabeth married Henry B. Longenecker, son of Christian and Fannie (Brenneman) Longenecker. Henry was born December 19, 1818 in Conoy Township, Lancaster County, Pa. He died on March 22, 1870 in Conoy Township "by the fall of a tree." Henry is buried with his wife in Good's Mennonite Cemetery.

Issue:

    i. Samuel E., b. July 4, 1855; d. September 22, 1934. Samuel married October 30, 1877 to Susan Lehman.

    ii. Esther who married Henry Landis

    iii. Christian who married Mary Hernley

    iv. Fannie who married John Burkholder

    v. David who married Barbara Lehman

    vi. Henry E., b. April 9, 1853 in West Donegal Township. Henry January 14, 1875 to Catherine Bomberger

    vii. Lizzie, d. unmarried

    viii. Annie who married Jacob Landis

    ix. John married Lizzie Hershey

    x. Amanda, d. unmarried

    xi. Abraham, b. 1870 in Conoy Township. Abraham married Lizzie Ebersole on January 5, 1893.

References:

Gerberich, Albert H., *The Brenneman History*, p. 74

History of Longacre - Longaker - Longenecker Family, pp. 135, 136 137

Inscriptions, Good's Mennonite Cemetery, near Elizabethtown, Pa.

Pennsylvania Mennonite Heritage, Vol. 6, No. 1, pp. 7 - 21
Ibid., Vol. 7, No. 1, p. 39

27. MARY B. EBERSOLE [David M.[3], Jacob[2], Jacob[1]], daughter of David M. and Elizabeth (Burkholder) Lehman Ebersole was born in 1827, probably in Conoy Township, Lancaster County, Pa. Her date and place of death are not now known.

Mary B. Ebersole was married to Abraham Burkholder, son of Abraham and Elizabeth (Whisler) Burkholder.

Issue:
  i. Lizzie E., b. July 22, 1857 in Lancaster County, Pa.
     d. June 11, 1916. Lizzie married Jacob H. Greiner.

References:
Mennonite Research Journal, Vol. III, No. 4, p. 48
Pennsylvania Mennonite Heritage, Vol. V, No. 3, p. 11

28. SAMUEL D. EBERSOLE [David M.[3], Jacob[2], Jacob[1]], son of David M. and Elizabeth (Burkholder) Lehman Ebersole was born October 21, 1829 at Elizabethtown, Lancaster County, Pa. He died at Elizabethtown September 14, 1896 and is buried at Good's Mennonite Cemetery, near Elizabethtown, Pa.

Samuel D. Ebersole married twice. His first wife was Susanna Burkholder who was born October 16, 1826. She died June 28, 1889 and is buried in Good's Mennonite Cemetery.

Issue:
  i. Mary B. married a man with the surname of Fetter.
  ii. Annie B., b. November 20, 1855; d. March 26, 1940.
  iii. Elias B., d. March 31, 1862
68. iv. Daniel B., b. October 5, 1863
  v. Elizabeth B., b. November 12, 1854; d. November 23, 1854 Bur. Good's Mennonite Cemetery.
  vi. Susanna B. b. May 24, 1860; d. October 10, 1860.   Bur. Good's Mennonite Cemetery.
  vii. Samuel B., b. April 6, 1861; d. April 6, 1861. Bur. Good's Mennonite Cemetery.

After the death of his first wife, Samuel married a second time to Sarah ____ on February 7, 1892. Samuel's second wife "Sally" may have been an Ebersole since the application for a marriages certificate notes "we are related

but it is very remote." Sarah's first husband died April 28, 1873.
    Samuel was a flour and feed dealer.
        References:
Burkholder Family Reunion Booklet, 1928, p. 29
Gerberich, Albert H., *Collection, Gravestone Inscriptions*, Microfilm Reel
        2, Part 2, p. 187
Herald of Truth, October 15, 1896
Inscriptions, Good's Mennonite Cemetery, near Elizabethtown, Pa.
Lancaster County, Pa. Orphans Court, Marriage Docket, Book M,
        License No. 7095
Lancaster County, Pa. Wills, Will of Samuel D. Ebersole Will Book M,
        Vol. 2, p. 37

29. DAVID B. EBERSOLE [David M.[3], Jacob[2], Jacob[1]], son of David
M. and Esther (Burkholder) Lehman Ebersole was born April 9, 1832 in
Conoy Township, Lancaster County, Pa. He died April 9, 1908.
    On November 2, 1854 David married Anna (also Annie) Martin at
Lancaster, Pa.
        Issue:
                i. Adaline b, September 18, 1855 in Lancaster County,   Pa.
                    d. June 19, 1910 at Sterling, Illinois and is buried in the
                    Sterling, Illinois Mennonite Cemetery.
                ii. Melinda, b. August 20, 1860 at Elizabethtown, Lancaster
                    County, Pa. d. March 6, 1933 at Sterling, Illinois and is
                    buried in the Science Ridge Cemetery at Sterling.
                iii. Ephraim, b. April 29, 1862 in Lancaster County, Pa.   d.
                    November 6, 1906 at Sterling, Illinois and is buried in the
                    Sterling Cemetery. m. Hattie Mack. Issue: Charles O., b.
                    1892 and Florence Marie, b. 1898.
69.   iv. David M., b. September 3, 1866
                v. Amanda
                vi. Anna
                vii. Mrs. A. W. Book
        References:
Davis Whiteside County Illustrated History, pp. 525, 1015
Gospel Herald, February 26, 1926, p. 991 July 7, 1910, p. 223 March 23,
        1933, p. 1087

30. CHRISTIAN K. EBERSOLE [Jacob M.³, Jacob², Jacob¹], son of
Jacob M. and Veronica (Mellinger) Ebersole was born April 13, 1823 in
Lancaster County, Pa. He died February 21, 1901 and is buried in the
Ebersole family cemetery, near Bainbridge, Pa.

December 13, 1842 Christian K. Ebersole was married to Mary Rutt
Ebersole, daughter of Peter R. and Mary (Rutt) Ebersole. Mary's father,
Peter R. Ebersole, was a Mennonite Bishop.

Issue: (all born in Lancaster County, Pa.)

70.   i. Peter C., b. November 26, 1843
             ii. Jacob C., b. November 9, 1845; d. September 2, 1929.
                 Bur. Good's Mennonite Cemetery. Jacob married Mary
                 D. Myers, b. November 20, 1844; d. April 12, 1915.
                 Bur. Good's Mennonite Cemetery. No issue.
            iii. Annie C., b. August 20, 1847; d. March 1, 1921. Annie
                 married Ephraim Risser.
71.   iv. Christian C., b. July 2, 1850.
              v. Barbara C., b. September 21, 1853; d. April 2, 1913.
                 Barbara married Henry L. Meyer (also Myers) on September
                 28, 1871 at Elizabethtown, Pa.
72.   vi. David C., b. January 15, 1857
            vii. Mary C., b. November 19, 1850. Mary was married April
                 20, 1890 to Abram A. Gall at Elizabethtown, Pa..
           viii. Henry C., b. October 10, 1863; d. October 16, 1874

References:
Gerberich, Albert H., *Gravestone Inscriptions, Good's Mennonite Meeting
    House*
Inscriptions, Good's Mennonite Cemetery, near Elizabethtown, Pa.
Lancaster County, Pa. Wills, Will of Jacob C. Ebersole, Will Book J, Vol.
3,
    p. 114
Records of Christ Lutheran Church, Elizabethtown, Pa.
Retherford, Audrey L, *Cemetery Records, etc.*
U. S. Census, 1850, Pennsylvania, Lancaster County, Conoy Township, p.
301
Records of Christ Lutheran Church, Elizabethtown, Pa., translated and
    transcribed by Frederick S. Weiser, p. 342

31. HENRY K. EBERSOLE [Jacob M.³, Jacob², Jacob¹], son of Jacob

M. and Barbara (Kauffaman) Ebersole was born November 5, 1830 in Conoy
Township, Lancaster County, Pa. He died April 24, 1873 in Conoy
Township and is buried in Good's Mennonite Cemetery, near Elizabethtown,
Pa.

Henry married a woman by the name of Sarah A._____, better known
as Sally. She was born July 18, 1833/34 and died January 31, 1905. After
Henry's death, Sally married Samuel Ebersole.

Issue:

  i. Sarah, b. February 4, 1855; d. January 18, 1936. Bur.
     Kraybill Mennonite Cemetery, Mt. Joy, Pa. on the same
     block as Henry K. Ebersole. Was there more than one
     Henry K. Ebersole?
  ii. Samuel H., b. February 19, 1860; d. October 14, 1891.
     Bur. Good's Mennonite Cemetery.
  iii. A daughter who died in 1863
  iv. A son who died November 24, 1866
  v. Jacob
  vi. Barbara
  vii. Anna who married Benjamin Shenk.
  viii. Elizabeth

References:

Gerberich, Albert H., *Gravestone Inscriptions, Good's Cemetery,*
   Microfilm Reel 2, Part 2, p. 187
Herald of Truth, March 2, 1905, p. 71
Inscriptions, Good's Mennonite Cemetery, Elizabethtown, Pa.
Lancaster County Orphans Court Records, Miscellaneous Book 1873 -
   1875, pp. 258, 628, 630
Ibid., Miscellaneous Book 1872 - 1873, pp. 518, 598
   "   Bond Book A, Vol. 2, p. 45
   "   Bond Book H, Vol. 2, p. 258
Lancaster County Deeds, Book N, Vol. 11, p. 20
Ibid., Book A, Vol. 12, p.456
   "   Book Q, Vol. 11, p. 330

32. JOSEPH EBERSOLE [Jacob G.[3], [Christian], Jacob[1]], son of Jacob G.
and Anna (Rutt) Ebersole was born in East Donegal Township, Lancaster
County, Pa. on December 4, 1809. He died March 25, 1879 and is buried in
the Kraybill Mennonite Church Cemetery, west of Mt. Joy, Pa.

Joseph Ebersole was married to Anna Nissley, daughter of preacher Martin Nissley and his wife, Anna Witmer. Anna was born February 4, 1811 and died July 8, 1895. She is buried with her husband in the Kraybill Mennonite Cemetery.

Issue:

    i. Noah N., b. about 1837
    ii. Martin N., b. March 13, 1839; d. unmarried March 13, 1882.
    iii. Abraham, b. July 29, 1841; d. March 2, 1842. Bur. Kraybill Mennonite Cemetery.
72.   iv. Joseph N., b. about 1843
    v. Ephraim, b. June 15, 1848; d. April 25, 1849.
    vi. Anna who married Samuel Burkholder.

References:

Brubacher, Jacob N., *The Brubacher Genealogy in America*, p. 138
Herald of Truth, June 1879, p. 117, April 1, 1882, p. 109
Inscriptions, Kraybill Mennonite Cemetery, near Mt. Joy, Pa.
Lancaster County, Pa. Deeds, Book E, Vol. 14, p. 547
Ibid., Book E, Vol. 8, p. 516
  "   Book D, Vol. 13, p. 271
Lancaster County Death Affidavits, Book B, Vol. , p. 154
Lancaster County Orphans Court Records, Bond Book G, Vol. 2, p. 50
Ibid., Accounts and Reports Book 68, p. 238
Lancaster County, Pa. Wills, Will of Anna Ebersole, Will Book L, Vol. 2, p. 299
Mennonite Research Journal, Vol. 3, No. 3, p. 36
New Era, Lancaster, Pa., July 31, 1895
U. S. Census, 1850, Pennsylvania, Lancaster County, East Donegal Township,

33. CHRISTIAN EBERSOLE [Jacob G.[3], Christian[2], Jacob[1]], son of Jacob G. and Anna (Rutt) Ebersole was born February 14, 1815 in Lancaster County, Pa. He died October 25, 1900 and is buried in the Kraybill Mennonite Cemetery, west of Mt. Joy, Lancaster County, Pa.

Christian married Nancy Kraybill who was born January 16, 1811 and died September 16, 1891. Nancy is buried with her husband in the Kraybill Cemetery.

Issue:

i. Peter, b. January 30, 1842; d. May 17, 1845. Bur. Kraybill Mennonite Cemetery.

ii. Annie K., b. May 29, 1845; d. unmarried May 17, 1916. Bur. Kraybill Mennonite Cemetery.

References:

Inscriptions, Kraybill Mennonite Cemetery, west of Mt. Joy, Pa.

Mennonite Research Journal, Vol. 3, No. 3, p. 36

34. SOLOMON R. EBERSOLE [Jacob G.³, Christian², Jacob¹], son of Jacob G. and Anna (Rutt) Ebersole was born November 15, 1822 at Lancaster, Pa. He died January 28, 1910 and is buried in the Neffsville Church of the Brethren Cemetery, Neffsville, Pa.

Solomon R. Ebersole married Sarah E. Diffenderfer.

Issue: (all born in Lancaster County, Pa.)

73.   i. Eli D., b. March 7, 1860

ii. Martin D., b. July 18, 1862

iii. Lizzie D., b. May 11, 1865. On December 25, 1887, Lizzie was married to John J. Parmer who was born in 1866 in Lancaster County, Pa. No known issue.

74.   iv. Solomon D., b. February 18, 1868

75.   v. Amos D., b. June 28, 1870

vi. Katie D., b. November 6, 1876; Katie was married February 23, 1897 to Charles D. Logan who was born in New York City in 1871.

vii. Ella D. (twin), b. May 25, 1879

viii. Amelia D. (twin), b. May 25, 1879

ix. Emma D., b. November 22, 1879. This is obviously an incorrect date. Perhaps she was born in 1877 or 1878.

76.   x. John D., b. 1889

References:

Hawbaker and Groff, *Cemetery Records, Frantz Graveyard and Neffsville Church of the Brethren,* Lancaster County Connections, Vol. 2, No. 2, p. 56

Lancaster County, Pa. Orphans Court, Marriage Docket, Vol. D, License No. 2453

Ibid., Marriages, Book W, License No. 12906

New Era, Lancaster, Pa., December 27, 1887

Parish and Vital Records Listings, The Genealogical Dept. of the Church

35. JOHN R. EBERSOLE [Jacob G.[3], Christian, Jacob[1]], son of Jacob G. and Anna (Rutt) Ebersole was born May 26, 1826 in Lancaster County, Pa. He died February 28, 1899 in Sterling, Illinois.

John R. Ebersole married Annie Rutt who was born July 4, 1829. She died September 16, 1905 and is buried with her husband at Sterling, Ill. Annie was the daughter of Samuel and Susanna (Whisler) Rutt.

Issue:

	i.	Samuel, b. 1849; d. in infancy.
77.	ii.	Jacob R., b. January 13, 1851; d. April 10, 1894.
	iii.	Martha, b. 1853; m. Henry Burkholder.
	iv.	Elizabeth H., b. April 8, 1856 near Elizabethtown, Pa. d. unmarried at Sterling, Ill. July 3, 1931.
	v.	Joseph R., b. about 1859. Joseph married Addie Over. Joseph R. Ebersole was a doctor.
	vi.	Anna R., b. May 1, 1863

References:
Gerberich, Albert H., *The Brenneman History,* p. 436
Gospel Herald, July 23, 1931, p. 399

36. PETER R. EBERSOLE [Peter R.[3], Christian[2], Jacob[1]], son of Peter R. and Mary (Risser) Ebersole was born April 2, 1822 in Lancaster County, Pa. He died January 23, 1899 in Conoy Township, Lancaster County, Pa. and is buried in Good's Mennonite Cemetery, near Elizabethtown, Lancaster County, Pa.

Peter married Susan Kendig. She was born September 6, 1825 and died June 6, 1900. Susan is buried at Good's Mennonite Cemetery with her husband.

Peter R. Ebersole was a Mennonite preacher.

Issue:

78.	i.	Mary, b. February 1846
	ii.	Veronica (Fanny), b. September 29, 1848; d. September 28, 1873. Bur. Good's Mennonite Cemetery.
79.	iii.	Martin K., b. 1851
80.	iv.	Peter K., b. April 1, 1853
	v.	Susan K., b. August 14, 1854; d. February 1, 1919. Bur. "Ebersole burying ground."

vi. Annie K., b. 1858. Annie married March 22, 1892 to
   Jesse Asper.

vii. John K., b. July 12, 1861

viii. Malinda, b. December 28, 1862; d. December 28, 1866.
   Bur. Ebersole Cemetery on Amosite Road, west of Good's
   Meeting House.

81.   ix. Amanda K., b. May 9, 1863. Amanda married October 2,
   1846 to Frank Landis.

82.   x. Elizabeth

References:

Beers, J. H. Co., *Biographical Annals of Lancaster County, Pa., p.*   *1361*

Gerberich, Albert H., *Collection of Gravestone Inscriptions, Ebersole*
   Burying Ground, p. 202

Herald of Truth, July 1, 1900, p. 206

Inscriptions, Ebersole Cemetery, on Amosite Road, about 1/2 mile west
   of Good's Mennonite Church, near Elizabethtown, Pa.

Lancaster County, Pa. Orphans Court, Marriage License Docket, Book
   M, License No. 7220

Mennonite Research Journal, Vol. V, No. 1, p. 2

Lancaster County Orphans Court Records, Bond Book T, Vol. 2, p. 254

Parish and Vital Records, The Genealogical Dept. of the Church of
   Jesus Christ of the Latter Day Saints (Microfiche Lists)

Retherford, Audrey L., *Cemetery Records of Conoy Township*   *(Lancaster*
   County, Pa.) Family Graveyards, 1979, p. 8

U. S. Census, 1850, Pennsylvania, Lancaster County, Conoy Township,
   p. 300

Landis, Frank K., Family Bible owned by Mrs. Anna E. Zeager,
   Elizabethtown, Pa.

Weaver, Martin G., *Mennonites of Lancaster County, etc.*

37. JACOB R. EBERSOLE [Peter R.[3], Christian[2], Jacob[1]], son of
Peter R. and Mary (Risser) Ebersole was born February 22, 1834 in
Lancaster County, Pa. He died April 15, 1913 in Conoy Township,
Lancaster County, Pa. and is buried in the Ebersole family cemetery on
Amosite Road, West of Good's Mennonite Church, near Elizabethtown, Pa.

Jacob married Anna R. Lehman, daughter of Peter Lehman, a farmer.
Anna was born January 16, 1834 and died September 29, 1897. She is
buried with her husband in the Ebersole family cemetery, west of Good's

Mennonite Church.
    Issue:
                i. Maria L., b. January 1, 1863; d. unmarried September
                    27, 1921. Bur. Ebersole family cemetery, west of
                    Good's Mennonite Church.
                ii. Elizabeth, b. November 11, 1859 in Conoy Township,
                    Lancaster County, Pa. d. unmarried March 24, 1861.
                    Bur. Ebersole family cemetery.
83.   iii. Peter L., b. 1856
                iv. "Son," d. October 1, 1858
84.   v. Jacob L., b. May 3, 1866
                vi. Annie, b. 1870; d. 1870 ???
    References:
Beers, J. H. & Co., *Biographical Annals of Lancaster County, Pa.*,
    p. 861
Gerberich, Albert H., *Collection of Gravestone Inscriptions,   Lancaster
    County, Pa., Ebersole Burying Ground,* Reel 2, Part 1, p. 202
Inscriptions, Ebersole Family Cemetery, on Amosite Road, west of
Lancaster County Wills, Will of Jacob R. Ebersole, Will Book V,
    Vol. 2, p. 342
Retherford, Audrey L., *Cemetery Records of Conoy Township
    (Lancaster County, Pa.) Family Graveyards, 1979, pp. 8, 10*
Good's Mennonite Church

38. JOHN FREY EBERSOLE [Christian R.³, Christian², Jacob¹], son
of Christian R. and Anna (Frey) Ebersole was born March 16, 1820 in
Franklin County, Pa. He died December 13, 1889 at Clarence Center, New
York and is buried in the Clarence Center Cemetery.
    John F. Ebersole married Nancy Horst who was born November 4, 1817
in Franklin County, Pa. She died October 24, 1905 and is buried in Marion
Mennonite Cemetery, Franklin County, Pa. It should be noted that some
records show her name as Anna.
    Issue:
85.   i. Henry H., b. 1842
86.   ii. Christian H., b. November 11, 1843
87.   iii. Levi D., b. May 3, 1846
                iv. A daughter; d. young
                v. A daughter; d. young

vi. A daughter; d. young

vii. Abraham L., b. August 11, 1860; d. February 19, 1895 at North Tonawanda, Niagara County, New York and is buried at the Clarence Center Cemetery, Clarence Center, New York

References:

Herald of Truth, November 16, 1905

Wenger, Samuel S., *The Wenger Book/A Foundation Book of American Wengers*, pp. 333, 643, 1059

Genealogical Card Catalog, Lancaster Mennonite Historical Society

39. SUSANNA EBERSOLE [John M.[3], Martin[2], Jacob[1]], daughter of John M. and Adaline (Weaver) Ebersole was born April 10, 1810 in Lancaster County, Pa. She died in May 22, 1888 in Conoy Township, Lancaster County and is buried in the Kraybill Mennonite Cemetery, near Mt. Joy, Pa.

Susanna (or Susan) was married to Abraham Eshelman who was born October 29, 1805 and who died in 1871. He, too, is buried in the Kraybill Mennonite Cemetery.

Issue:

i. Simon, b. September 7, 1855; Simon married (1) Mary A. Zeager. He married (2) Mary J. Arms.

ii. Ann, b. April 27, 1828; d. September 16, 1889. Ann married Levi L. Henry.

References:

Inscriptions, Kraybill Mennonite Cemetery, near Mt. Joy, Pa.

Mennonite Research Journal, Vol. 3, No. 4, p. 47

Ibid., Vol. 4, No. 1, p. 12

40. MARTIN EBERSOLE [John M.[3], Martin[2], Jacob[1]], son of John M. and Adaline (Weaver) Ebersole was born in Lancaster County, Pa. His dates of birth and death are not now known.

Martin Ebersole married Anne _____.

Issues: (all born in Conoy Township, Lancaster County, Pa.)

i. Elizabeth, b. 1843. She married Henry Deimler on July 17, 1864. Henry was b. April 27, 1829; d. January 6, 1924.

ii. Anne

iii. Martha

References:

Lancaster County Orphans Court Records, Miscellaneous Book 1848 -
    1850, p. 35

Ibid., Miscellaneous Book 1863 - 1865, p. 298

41. DANIEL EBERSOLE [Jacob³, Martin², Jacob¹], son of Jacob and
Fannie (Mellinger) Ebersole was born May 6, 1821 in Conoy Township,
Lancaster County, Pa. He died May 11, 1874 and is buried in Good's
Mennonite Cemetery, near Elizabethtown, Pa.

Daniel Ebersole married Elizabeth Ebersole, the daughter of Samuel W.
and Sarah (Shenk) Ebersole on December 5, 1844. Elizabeth was born in
1827 and died in 1912.

Daniel Ebersole was a farmer and a Mennonite preacher.

Issue:

	i. Anna, b. about 1846; d. young
88.	ii. Samuel E., b. January 12, 1847
89.	iii. Amos E., November 20, 1848
	iv. Ada, b. 1850; d. March 26, 1892
	v. Sarah, b. 1850 (Although listed in the 1850 census, Sarah may not be a daughter.)
	vi. Fanny, b. November 1, 1851; d. April 1, 1857
	vii. Barbara, b. July 22, 1855; d. November 22, 1861.
	viii. Daniel, b. May 16, 1857; d. July 16, 1864
90.	ix. Abraham E., b. November 6, 1858
91.	x. Jacob E., b. October 9, 1861

References:

Beers, J. H. & Co., *Biographical Annals of Lancaster County, Pa.*,
    p. 1362

Inscriptions, Good's Mennonite Cemetery

Lancaster County, Pa., Orphans Court Records, Accounts and Reports
    Book 42, p. 219

Ibid., Miscellaneous Book 1873 - 1875, p. 234
    Miscellaneous Book 1881 - 1182, p. 436
    Bond Book A, Vol. 2, p. 211, 213

Lancaster County, Pa., Deeds, Book B, Vol. 12, p. 319

Mennonite Research Journal, Vol. 5, No. 1, p. 2

Records of Christ Evangelical Lutheran Church, Elizabethtown, Pa.

Retherford, Audrey L., *Cemetery Records of Conoy Township (Lancaster County, Pa.) Family Graveyards, 1979,* p. 6

U. S. Census, 1850, Pennsylvania, Lancaster County, Mr. Joy Township, p. 17

Weaver, *Mennonites of Lancaster Conferences,* p. 212

42. DANIEL A. EBERSOLE [John M.[4], Jacob B.[3], John[2], Jacob[1]], son of John Moyer and Sarah (Arnold) Ebersole was born January 26, 1836 in Londonderry Township, Lebanon County, Pa. He died May 21, 1897 at Palmyra, Lebanon County, Pa. and is buried in the Salem Reformed Church Cemetery, Campbelltown, Lebanon County, Pa.

Daniel was married to Louisa Boltz on November 2, 1867 at Annville, Lebanon County, Pa. Louisa, daughter of Simon Boltz was born November 11, 1839 in North Annville Township, Lebanon County, Pa. She died August 27, 1881 and is buried with her husband at the Salem Reformed Church Cemetery in Campbelltown.

Daniel was a farmer in the vicinity of Campbelltown, Lebanon County, Pa.
Issue:

      i. Sarah Lizzie, b. July 4, 1869; d. April 8, 1885. Sarah is buried with her parents at Campbelltown.

References:

Ebersole, Daniel A., Family bible

Evening Report, Lebanon, Pa., May 22, 1897

Inscriptions, Salem Reformed Church Cemetery, Campbelltown, Lebanon   County, Pa.

Lebanon County, Pa. Wills, Will of Daniel A. Ebersole, Will Book H, p. 466

Lebanon Daily News, Lebanon, Pa., May 22, 1897

The Lebanon Courier, Lebanon, Pa., November 7, 1867

43. ELIZABETH A. EBERSOLE [John M.[4], Jacob B.[3], John[2], Jacob[1]], daughter of John Moyer and Sarah (Arnold) Ebersole was born July 1, 1837 in Londonderry Township, Lebanon County, Pa. She died September 13, 1867 and is buried at Gingrich's Mennonite Church, near Lebanon, Pa.

Elizabeth was married to Adam Witmeyer who was born October 20, 1836 and died December 12, 1879. He is buried with his wife at Gingrich's Mennonite Cemetery.

John A. Witmeyer wrote this account of his mother's death in *Descendants of .John A. Witmeyer and Sarah Snoke Witmeyer,* "One day Mother and the hired girl went to the mountains for blackberries and Mother was bitten from a rattlesnake and got so poisoned that the doctors could not take it all out of her system so she was sickly for two years and then died very young."

After the death of Elizabeth, Adam was married to Priscilla Yeagley. Nothing more is known about Priscilla.

During the years that Elizabeth was sickly her sister, Leah, "came to help with her care and the care of the children and to do the house work."

A note of interest. Adam and his wife, Elizabeth, were buried in a Mennonite cemetery even though they were members of Christ Reformed Church at Annville, Pa.

Issue:

92.   i. John A., b. October 16, 1860
        ii. Franklin E., b. September 26, 1863; d. March 21, 1864.
            Bur. Gingrich's Mennonite Church cemetery.
       iii. Emma

References:
Inscriptions, Gingrich's Mennonite Church Cemetery, Lebanon, Pa.
Witmeyer, John A., *History of the Witmeyer Family*
Witmeyer, John A. and Sarah Snoke Witmeyer, Descendants of John A.
    and Sarah Snoke Witmeyer, *Descendants of John A. and Sarah*
    Snoke Witmeyer
(Authors" s note: The pages of this family history are not numbered which makes the index useless.)_

44. JOHN A. EBERSOLE [JOHN M.[4], Jacob B.[3], John[2], Jacob[1]], son of John M. and Sarah (Arnold) Ebersole was born December 2, 1838 in Londonderry Township, Lebanon County, Pa. He died April 13, 1908 and is buried in the United Brethren Cemetery at Annville, Lebanon County, Pa.

On December 30, 1865 ,John A. Ebersole was married to Frany Moyer, daughter of Martin and Mary (Kreider) Moyer. Frany was born October 7, 1841. She died January 26, 1916 and is buried with her husband at the United Brethren Cemetery, Annville, Pa.

John Ebersole was a farmer who served two enlistments in the U. S. Army;

Of his two enlistments, one was with Company A, 48th Regiment, Pennsylvania Volunteers. He enlisted in Company A on July 2, 1863 and was honorably discharged August 25, 1863.

His second enlistment was with Company F, 93rd Regiment, Pennsylvania Volunteers. on February 29, 1864 at Reading, Berks County, Pa. He was honorably discharged from this regiment on June 27, 1865. Most of the men in this regiment were recruited from Lebanon County, Pennsylvania.

John's nephew, John A. Witmeyer, wrote that his uncle was captured by Confederate troops and imprisoned at Libby prison, Richmond, Virginia. He also told how the men were sitting in camp one day when they heard shots. His uncle. His uncle, John A. Ebersole, took a look around and noticed a black spot in a tree. He picked up his gun, fired and a sharpshooter dropped from the tree.

When John was discharged from the military, he bought his uniform from the government, brought it home and gave it to his nephew, James Ebersole.

John's obituary notes that he was a "Hoffmanite." The Hoffmanites were a splinter group of Mennonites founded in Europe.

Issue:

      i. George Monroe. The dates on the gravestone for George are so weathered that they are no longer legible. However, since the gravestone stands with John A. Ebersole and his wife, Frany, it is assumed that George Monroe Ebersole is their son..

References:

Ebersole family papers

Inscriptions, Untied Brethren Cemetery, Annville, Pa.

National Archives, Washington, D. C., Pension application of John A. Ebersole

Witmeyer, John A. and Sarah Snoke Witmeyer, *Descendants of John Adam Witmeyer and Sarah Snoke Witmeyer*

45. ELIAS A. EBERSOLE [John M.[4], Jacob B.[3], John[2], Jacob[1]], son of John M. and Sarah (Arnold) Ebersole was born March 19, 1840 in Londonderry Township, Lebanon County, Pa. He died February 19, 1915 and is buried at the Hanoverdale Church of the Brethren, Hanoverdale, Dauphin County, Pa.

Elias was married to Catherine Longenecker, the daughter of George and Magdalena (Hollinger) Longenecker.

Elias Ebersole was a farmer south of Palmyra, Pa. His farm was along the road to Campbelltown, Pa.

Issue:

i. Margaret, b. January 23, 1865; d. July 28, 1932 unmarried. Bur. with her parents at the Hanoverdale Cemetery.

93.   ii. Henry Clinton Longenecker, b. September 1, 1866

94.   iii. Allen Longeneckeer, b. February 5, 1868

95.   iv. Emma Longenecker, b. September 1, 1869

v. Jonas Longenecker, b. February 77, 1871; d. December 9, 1939 unmarried. Bur. at the Hanoverdale Cemetery. Jonas was a farmer.

96.   vi. Elizabeth Longenecker, b. August 3, 1872

vii. Amos, d. January 17, 1876; d. January 17, 1878. Bur. Spring Creek Cemetery, Hershey, Dauphin County, Pa.

97.   viii. Susan P., b. June 15, 1874

98.   ix. Isaac L., b, November 27, 1883

References:

Ebersole, Clinton L., family bible

Heilman, F. Irene Ebersole, Personal interview

Inscriptions, Hanoverdale Church of the Brethren Cemetery, Hanoverdalel, Dauphin County, Pa.

Inscriptions, Salem Reformed Church Cemetery, Campbelltown, Pa.

Longenecker, George, Family bible

46. MARY A. EBERSOLE [John M.[4], Jacob B.[3], John[2], Jacob[1]], daughter of John M. and Sarah (Arnold) Ebersole was born February 7, 1843 in Londonderry Township, Lebanon County, Pa. She died June 16, 1923 at Annville, Pa. and is buried at the Salem Reformed Cemetery, Campbelltown, Lebanon County, Pa.

On November 28, 1868, Mary was married to Jacob K. Shenk. Jacob was born February 14, 1846 and died March 23, 1915. He is buried with his wife at the Salem Reformed Cemetery.

Mary's husband was a successful merchant and realtor.

Issue:

i. Minerva E., b. December 25, 1872 at Annville, Lebanon County, Pa. She died January 4, 1959 at Lebanon, Lebanon County, Pa. Bur. with her parents at Campbelltown, Pa. Minerva married April 1, 1890 to

Dr. W. R. Dohner from whom she was divorced after a brief marriage.

References:

Died Lebanon Volks=Zeitung, Lebanon, Pa., April 16, 1890
Ebersole family papers now in the possession of Robert A. Heilman
Inscriptions, Salem Reformed Church cemetery, Campbelltown, Pa.
Shenk, Jacob K., Family bible
The Lebanon Courier, Lebanon, Pa., December 3, 1868

47. JACOB A. EBERSOLE [John M.[4], Jacob B.[3], John[2], Jacob[1]], son of John M. and Sarah (Arnold) Ebersole was born May 23, 1850 in Londonderry Township, Lebanon County, Pa. He died March 31, 1929 at Palmyra, Pa. and is buried at the Gravel Hill Cemetery, Palmyra, Pa.

August 17, 1872, Jacob was married to Mary Ann Emerich, daughter of George and Elizabeth (Farling) Emerich. Mary Ann was born December 10, 1850 in South Annville Township, Lebanon County, Pa. She died November 7, 1926 and is buried with her husband at the Gravel Hill Cemetery.

Jacob A. Ebersole was both a farmer and a saw mill worker.

Issue:

      i. James E., b. November 27, 1875 at Bethel, Berks County, Pa. He died February 5, 1920 and is buried at the Gravel Hill Cemetery, Palmyra, Pa. James married Nell Hill, daughter of the Confederate General A. P. Hill. No known issue.

99.   ii. Sadie, b. April 30, 1877

      iii. Ralph E., b. September 12, 1881 at "Hebrewsnoch," Lebanon County, Pa.

      iv. Mabel Bessie, b. March 14, 1888 at Bellegrove, Lebanon County, Pa. d. March 17, 1964 unmarried. Bur. Gravel Hill Cemetery, Palmyra, Pa.

References:

Ebersole family papers now in the possession of Robert A. Heilman
Inscriptions, Bellegrove U. B. Church Cemetery, Bellegrove, Lebanon County, Pa.
Inscriptions, Gravel Hill Cemetery, Palmyra, Pa.
Lebanon County, Pa. Wills, Will of Jacob A. Ebersole, Will Book N, p. 145
Lebanon Daily News, Lebanon, Pa., March 17, 1964

48. ELIZABETH GISH EBERSOLE [Jacob M.[4], Jacob B.[3], John[2], Jacob[1]], daughter of Jacob Moyer and Barbara (Gish) Ebersole was born June 30, 1846 at Palmyra, Lebanon County, Pa. Her date of death is not now known. She is buried at the Mt. Tunnel Cemetery, Elizabethtown, Pa.

Elizabeth was married to John H. Boyer on January 11, 1870. John, son of Joseph and Mary (Herr) Boyer, was born March 17, 1843. He died March 11, 1915 and is buried with his wife at the Mt. Tunnel Cemetery.

Issue:

  i. Harry E., b. March 6, 1870 in Lancaster County, Pa. He died November 21, 1886 and is buried tat the Mt. Tunnel Cemetery. Elizabethtown, Pa.

References:

Boyer, Charles C., *American Boyers*, p. 426
Inscriptions, Mt. Tunnel Cemetery, Elizabethtown, Pa.
The Lebanon Courier, Lebanon, Pa., February 3, 1870

49. BARBARA GISH EBERSOLE [Jacob M.[4], Jacob B.[3], John[2], John[1]], daughter of Jacob M. and Barbara (Gish) Ebersole was born November 27, 1847 in Londonderry Township, Lebanon County, Pa. She died July 15, 1907 and is buried at the Gravel Hill Cemetery, Palmyra, Lebanon County, Pa.

On September 14, 1865, Barbara was married to Adam Naftzger at Annville, Lebanon County, Pa. Adam was born March 9, 1842. He died August 18, 1911 and is buried with his wife at the Gravel Hill Cemetery.

Issue:

  i. John A., b. April 23, 1867; d. March 22, 1950. John was married to Dora H. Garman. Dora was born October 23, 1872 and died October 20, 1940

  ii. Joseph, b. November 4, 1872; d. June 25, 1904.

  iii. Carrie M., b. December 8, 1893; d. February 12, 1904..

  iv. Elizabeth (Lizzie) who married a man whose surname was Bowman.

  v. Clayton, b.

References:

Gerberich, Albert H., *Gravestone Inscriptions* (Microfilm), Reel 1, Part 1, p. 322
Inscriptions, Gravel Hill Cemetery, Palmyra, Pa.
Records of Christ Reformed Church, Annville, Pa.

50. JOHN GISH EBERSOLE [Jacob M.[4], Jacob B.[3], John[2], Jacob[1]], son of Jacob M. and Barbara (Gish) Ebersole was born January 28, 1849 at Hockersville, Dauphin County, Pa. He died February 19, 1934 at Lawn, Lebanon County, Pa. and is buried at Stauffer's Mennonite Church, Bachmanville, Dauphin County, Pa.

John G. Ebersole was married to Sylvanus A. Hatton December 26, 1872 at Derry Church (now Hershey), Dauphin County, Pa. Sylvanus was born June 29, 1851 and died October 25, 1919 at Lawn, Lebanon County, Pa. She is buried with her husband in the churchyard of Stauffer's Mennonite Church. Nothing more is now known of Sylvanus (also Sylvania).

John G. Ebersole was a Bishop in the Mennonite Church and served congregations in both Lancaster and Lebanon Counties. He was first ordained as a preacher in June of 1887 and was later chosen, by lot, as a Bishop on August 22, 1907 at Elizabethtown, Lancaster County, Pa.

Issue:

100.	i.	Elizabeth, b. October 18, 1873
101.	ii.	Moses H., b. January 6, 1876
102.	iii.	Susanna H., b. September 14, 1878
	iv.	Daniel H., b. January 12, 1882; d. June 1, 1913. Bur. Stauffer's Mennonite Church.
	v.	Mary H., b. April 3, 1884 at Colebrook, Lebanon County, Pa. She died June 27, 1898 and is buried at Stauffer's Mennonite Church.
	vi.	Anna H., b. March 25, 1886 at Lawn, Lebanon County, Pa. She died December 28, 1966. Anna was married May 17, 1921 to Philip Honafius, son of George and Harriet (Lowery) Honafius. Philip was born about 1892. Anna and Philip were divorced by the Lebanon County, Pa. Courts on May 7, 1931. After the divorce Anna used her maiden name, No known issue.
103.	vii.	John H., b. August 1, 1889
	viii.	Jacob H., b. January 25, 1892; d. 30 April 1972 at York, York County, Pa. He married September 6, 1924 to Alverta Flinchbaugh. Alverta preceded Jacob in death. no known issue. Despite his Mennonite upbringing, Jacob was a member of the Red Lion United Methodist Church, Red Lion, York County, Pa.
104.	ix.	Phoebe H., b. April 4, 1894

References:
Ebersole, John G., Family bible
Inscriptions, Stauffer's Mennonite Church, Bachmanville, Dauphin
     County, Pa.
Lebanon County, Pa. Index of Divorces, p. H-8
Lebanon County, Pa. Register of Births
Lebanon County, Pa. Register of Deaths
Lebanon County, Pa. Wills, Will of John G. Ebersole, Will Book M,
     Vol. 3, p. 375
Lebanon Daily News, Lebanon, Pa., 1 May 1972
Pennsylvania Mennonite Heritage, Vol. VI, No. 1, pp. 18, 19

51. JACOB MOYER EBERSOLE [Jacob M.[4], Jacob B.[3], John[2], Jacob[1]], son of Jacob M. and Mary (Moyer) Ebersole was born July 1, 1854 in Lancaster County, Pa. He died April 19, 1946 in Rapho Township, Lancaster County, Pa. and is buried at Risser's Mennonite Church, east of Elizabethtown, Pa.

Jacob was married to Annie C. Ebersole, daughter of Daniel M. Ebersole and his wife, Lydia Keenports. Annie was born December 13, 1866 and died February 19, 1953. She is buried at Risser's cemetery with her husband.

    Issue:
> i. Ellen R., b. January 31, 1871; d. March 25, 1880. Bur. at Risser's Mennonite Church.
> ii. Daniel B., b. April 27, 1872; d. March 3, 1849. Bur. at Risser's.
> iii. _____, b. October 22, 1874; d. March 26, 1892.

References:
Inscriptions, Risser's Mennonite Church Cemetery, near Elizabethtown,
    Pa.
Lancaster County, Pa. Wills, Will of Jacob M. Ebersole, Book W,
    Vol. 3, p. 173
Lancaster County, Pa. Wills, Will of Annie C. Ebersole, Book C,
    Vol. 4, p. 129

52. SAMUEL MOYER EBERSOLE [Jacob M.[4], Jacob B.[3], John[2], Jacob[1]], son of Jacob M. and Mary (Moyer) Ebersole was born April 28, 1864 at Palmyra, Lebanon County, Pa. He died April 11, 1944 in Rapho Township, Lancaster County, Pa. and is buried at Risser's Mennonite

Cemetery, near Elizabethtown, Pa.

On December 14, 1893, Samuel was married to Isabella F. Gruber. Isabella was born February 5, 1871 in Mt. Joy Township, Lancaster County, Pa. She died October 1, 1898 and is buried with her husband at Risser's Mennonite Cemetery.

Issue:

105.   i. Mary G., b. April 27, 1896

After the death of Isabella, Samuel married Lizzie W. Enterline on August 28, 1900. Lizzie was born March 19, 1868 in Warwick Township, Lancaster County, Pa. She died January 6, 1922 and is buried at Risser's Mennonite Cemetery.

Issue:

    ii. Amos E., b. November 20, 1902 at Lawn, Lebanon County, Pa. He died November 27, 1902 and is buried at Risser's Mennonite Cemetery.

    iii. John E., b. June 12, 1905 in Mt. Joy Township, Lancaster County, Pa. On November 22, 1924 John was married to Rhoda F. Ginder, daughter of Abram F. and Lizzie L. (Fisher) Ginder. They were married at Lawn, Lebanon County, Pa. by Mennonite Bishop John G. Ebersole. Rhoda was born about 1905 in Mt. Joy Township, Lancaster County, Pa.

    iv. Elizabeth, b. 1909 in Mt. Joy Township, Lancaster County, Pa. Elizabeth was married to Daniel H. Rhoade on January 20, 1913.

Samuel married a third time on June 5, 1924 when he married Mary A. Lefever, daughter of Abram Newcomer and Mary Root, at Lawn, Lebanon County, Pa. Mary was born in Manor Township, Lancaster County, Pa. about the year 1878. Her former husband had died on February 17, 1920. No known issue from this marriage.

Bertha Heller, daughter of Henry L. and Fanny (Rohrer) Heller, became Samuel's fourth wife on May 15, 1930. Bertha was born August 26, 1880 and died July 22, 1933. She is buried at the Landis Valley Cemetery, near Neffsville, Pa. She was formerly married to Harry Boose. No known issue from this marriage either.

References:

Inscriptions, Landis Valley Cemetery, near Neffsville, Pa.
Inscriptions, Risser's Mennonite Cemetery, near Elizabethtown, Pa.

Lancaster County, Pa. Orphans Court, Marriage License Docket,, Book Q,
    License No. 9249
Ibid., Book F, Vol. 2, Certificate No. 17068
  "   Book F, Vol. 5, Certificate No. 2621
  "   Book U, Vol. 5, Certificate No. 10210
Lancaster County, Pa. Record of Births
Lancaster County, Pa. Wills, Will of Samuel M. Ebersole, Will Book   U,
    Vol. 3, p. 248
Lebanon County, Pa. Register of Deaths

53. DAVID MOYER EBERSOLE [Jacob M.[4], Jacob B.[3], John[2], Jacob[1]], son of Jacob M. and Mary (Moyer) Ebersole was born May 26, 1867 at Derry Church (now Hershey), Dauphin County, Pa. He died December 24, 1951 and is buried at the Mt. Pleasant Brethren in Christ Cemetery, Mt. Joy, Lancaster County, Pa.

On January 11, 1890, David M. Ebersole was married to Alice S. Brandt at Beverly, Lancaster County, Pa. Alice, daughter of Peter Brandt was born in 1872 at Elizabethtown, Pa. She died January 5, 1928 at Mt. Joy, Pa. and is buried with her husband at the Mt. Pleasant Brethren in Christ Cemetery. Her tombstone records her date of death as 1934.

David was a lime burner.

Issue:

i. Anna Mary. Anna married Amos Sipling.

ii. Mabel M., b. 1894 at Middletown, Dauphin County, Pa. Mabel married 4 September 1910 to Isaac Geib who was born in 1879 at Mt. Joy, Lancaster County, Pa.

iii. Bertha N., b. 1899 at Middletown, Dauphin County, Pa. Bertha was married January 18, 1917 to John S. Heisey who was born in 1897.

106. iv. Lloyd B., b. 1902 at Middletown, Pa.

v. Martha, b. 1909 in Lancaster County, Pa. On August 12, 1926 Martha was married to Norman C. Shenk at Mt. Joy, Lancaster County, Pa. Norman was born in 1905 in Lancaster County, Pa.

References:
Gospel Herald, January 15, 1952
Gravestone Inscriptions, Mt. Pleasant Brethren in Christ Cemetery, Mt. Joy,
    Pa.

Heisey, M. Luther, *The Heisey Family in America,*, p. 70

Inscriptions, Mt. Pleasant Brethren in Christ Cemetery, near Mt. Joy, Pa.

Lancaster County, Pa. Orphans Court, Marriage License Docket Vol. H, Certificate No. 4720

Ibid., Book I, Vol. 4, License No. 4693

" Book K, Vol. 5, License No. 5227

Lancaster County, Pa. Wills, Will of Alice Brandt Ebersole, Will Book H, Vol. 3, p. 225

Ibid., Book R, Vol. 3, License No. 4385

54. JOHN B. EBERSOLE [Daniel M.[4], Jacob B.[3], John[2], Jacob[1]], son of Daniel M. and Lydia (Keenports) Ebersole was born October 4, 1863 in Lancaster County, Pa. His date and place of death are not now known.

On March 25, 1890, John was married to Margaret Shuman. Margaret, the daughter of Eli and Elizabeth (Mann) Shuman was born July 22. 1858 and died January 11, 1934.

Issue:

      i. Christian Seidel, b. May 3, 1891
      ii. Margaret Shuman, b. January 30, 1893; d. May 16, 1894.
      iii. Constance
      iv. Paul L.
      v. John W.

References:

Gerberich, Albert H., *The Brenneman History*, p. 213

Shuman, William C., *The George Shuman Family Genealogy and History from the Time of Arrival in America, in 1760, to the year 1913*, p. 182

55. MARY MOYER EBERSOLE [Daniel M.[4], Jacob B.[3], John[2], Jacob[1]], daughter of Daniel M. and Lydia (Keenports) Ebersole was born July 13, 1869. Her date and place of death are not now known.

Mary Moyer Ebersole was married to Harry M. Nickel.

Issue:

      i. Earl Wayne, b. September 10, 1904; d. June 21, 1911.
      ii. Erma May, married Walden Wheeler.

References:

Records of Tabor Reformed Church, Lebanon, Pa.

56. BARBARA L. EBERSOLE [John D.[4], David[3], Jacob[2], Jacob[1]], daughter of John D. and Fanny B. (Longenecker) Ebersole was born March 12, 1839 in Lancaster County, Pa. She died September 16, 1927.

Barbara was married to Abraham Rutt. Abraham was born November 16, 1837 and died March 21, 1898.

Issue:
  i. Ellen who married Martin Metzger
  ii. Edwin who married Lizzie Gruber
  iii. Fannie married Michael Mumma
  iv. Barbara
  v. Abraham who married Lizzie Fink

In addition to the children named above, there were two who died in childhood.

References:
Gerberich, Albert H., *The Brenneman History*, p. 74
History of the Longacre - Longaker - Longenecker Family, pp. 130 - 133

57. LEVI L. EBERSOLE [John D.[4], David[3], Jacob[2], Jaocb[1]], son of John D. and Fanny B. (Longenecker) Ebersole, was born July 26, 1840 in Lancaster County, Pa. He died October 8, 1920 at Elizabethtown, Lancaster County, Pa. and is buried in Good's Mennonite Cemetery, near Elizabethtown, Pa.

Levi was married to Mary N. Risser, daughter of Joseph and Fanny (Nissley) Risser. Mary was born July 19, 1848 and died April 15, 1934. She is buried with her husband at Good's Mennonite Cemetery.

Levi L. Ebersole was a farmer and an ordained Mennonite preacher.

Issue: (all born in Lancaster County, Pa.)
  i. Tillman R., b. September 16, 1867. He died May 6, 1880 and is buried at Good's Mennonite Cemetery with his parents.
107.   ii. Amos R., b. December 22, 1870
108.   iv. Fannie R., b. 1876
  v. Emma, b. 1877 in Conoy Township; Emma was married December 24, 1898 to Addison J. Martin at Elizabethtown, Pa. Addison was born in 1876 in Mt. Joy Township, Lancaster County, Pa.

109.   v. Martin R., b. February 8, 1879
           vi. John R., single
   Levi L. Ebersole was an ordained Mennonite preacher. His ordination took place in the spring of 1875.
   References:

Beers, J. H. & Co., *Biographical Annals of Lancaster County, Pa.,*
      p. 1146
Gerberich, Albert H., *The Brenneman History,* p. 74
Gerberich, Albert H., *Gravestone Inscriptions, Good's Mennonite*
      Meeting House, West Donegal Township
History of Longacre - Longaker - Longenecker Family, pp. 131 - 133
Inscriptions, Good's Mennonite Cemetery, near Elizabethtown, Pa.
Lancaster County, Pa. Wills, Will of Levi L. Longenecker, Will Book B,
      Vol. 3, p. 544
Weaver, Martin G., *Mennonites of Lancaster Conference,* p. 213

   58. ANNA EBERSOLE [John D.[4], David M.[3], Jacob[2], Jacob[1]], daughter of John David and Fanny (Longeneceker) Ebersole, was born June 24, 1843. Her date and place of death are not now known.
   Annie, as she was better known, was the wife of Abraham Risser, the son of John and Mary (Shenk) Risser. He was born October 20, 1838 at Lawn, Lebanon County, Pa. He died December 25, 1876.
   Issue:
       i. Elias who married Rosie Gingrich.
       ii. Amanda who married Seth Brubaker. After the death of Seth, Amanda married a second time to John Snyder. She had five children from her first husband and none from the second husband.
   References:

Beers, J. H. Co., *Biographical Annals of Lebanon County, Pa.,* p. 206
Gerberich, Albert H., *The Brenneman History, p. 74*
History of the Longaker - Longacre - Longenecker Family, pp. 130-   133

   59 DAVID L. EBERSOLE [John D.[4], David M.[3], Jacob[2], Jacob[1]], son of John David and Fanny (Longenecker) Ebersole, was born August 14, 1844 in Lancaster County, Pa. He died in Freeport, Illinois February 14, 1899.
   David was married to Maria Brubaker, daughter of Rudolph Brubaker and

Elizabeth Sechrist. She was born April 8, 1849 and died June 17, 1942.
Issue:
>   i. Ella, b. December 25, 1873. Ella married Arthur Ritzman, b. July 10, 1870.
>   ii. Annie, b. 1877; d. 1903.
>   iii. Cora Frances, b. January 19, 1883. Cora married Tillman (also Dilman) S. Gingrich, b. October 8, 1875
>   iv. Fanny, b. November 23, 1886; Fanny married Fred N. Burkey, b. September 25, 1884.

References:
Freeport Daily Bulletin, Freeport, Illinois, August 30, 1899
Gerberich, Albert H., *The Brenneman History,* p. 74
Gospel Herald, July 23, 1942, p. 366
Herald of Truth, March 1, 1899, p. 77
History of the Longacre - Longaker - Longenecker Family, p. 132

60. ELIZABETH EBERSOLE [John D.[4], David M.[3], Jacob[2], Jacob[1]], daughter of John David and Fanny (Longenecker) Ebersole, was born February 12, 1852. She died March 28, 1932.

Elizabeth (also known as Lizzie) was married to Martin N. Mumma, son of Christian and Nancy (Nissley) Mumma. Elizabeth was the second wife of Martin Mumma who had been previously married to Elizabeth Bergey.

Martin Mumma was a Mennonite preacher and quite likely a farmer.
Issue:
>   i. Anna E., b. August 11, 1879; d. October 6, 1923. On October 5, 1905 Anna was married to Edward M. Snavely.
>   ii. Martin L., b. 1833; d. 1950. Martin was married January 21, 1915 to Nellie M. Beck.
>   iii. Mary E., b. October 3, 1885; d. unmarried August 25, 1974.

References:
Gerberich, Albert H., *The Brenneman History,* p. 74
Pennsylvania Mennonite Heritage, Vol. 6, No. 1, p. 17

61 ELIAS RUTT EBERSOLE [Abraham B.[4], David M.[3], Jacob[2], Jacob[1]], son of Abraham B. and Anna E. (Rutt) Ebersole, was born January 8, 1847 in Lancaster County, Pa. He died August 20, 1914 at Wakarusa,

Indiana.

Elias was married twice. his first wife, whom he married on February 21, 1872, was Barbara Buckwalter Stauffer. Barbara was born January 11, 1852. She died January 11, 1895 in Adams County, Nebraska and is buried in the Roselan, Nebraska Mennonite Church Cemetery.

Issue:

    i. Kate, b. October 19, 1873
    ii. Frank S., b. November 28, 1875
    iii. Reuben R., b. February 28, 1878
    iv. Esther, b. June 26, 1880
    v, William C., b. February 12, 1883
    vi. Mary, b. December 22, 1886
    vii. Benjamin S., b. May 7, 1890

After the death of Barbara, Elias married a second time to Leah A. Horning. Leah was born January 13, 1862 and died March 13, 1922. Bur. Olive Cemetery, Sterling, Illinois.

References:
Gospel Herald, June 1, 1922, p. 175
Umble, John, *Descendants of Preacher Abraham Burkholder Ebersole and his Wife, Anna Ebersole Rutt.*

62 ESTHER (HETTIE) EBERSOLE [Abraham B.[4], David M.[3], Jacob[2], Jacob[1]], daughter of Abraham B. and Anna E. (Rutt) Ebersole was born January 18, 1849 in Lancaster County, Pa. She died March 8, 1926 in Sterling, Illinois and is buried at the Science Ridge Cemetery.

On December 16, 1869, Esther was married to John J. Byers at Sterling, Ill. John was born May 28, 1844 and died April 17, 1874 at Sterling, Ill. He is buried at the Science Ridge Cemetery, Sterling, Ill with his wife.

Issue: (both born at Sterling, Illinois)

    i. John J. Jr., b. April 27, 1871
    ii. Noah E., b. July 26, 1873

        Both John and Noah are buried at Sterling, Ill.

References:
Umble, John, *Descendants of Preacher Abraham Burkholder Ebersole and his Wife, Anna Ebersole Rutt.*

63. MAGDALENA EBERSOLE [Abraham B.[4], David M.[3], Jacob[2], Jacob[1]], daughter of Abraham B. and Anna E. (Rutt) Ebersole, was born

March 9, 1851 in Lancaster County, Pa. She died in 1892 at Sterling, Illinois and is buried in the Science Ridge Cemetery at Sterling.

On December 24, 1870, Magdalena was married to John Kreider, a farmer, at Sterling, Ill.

Issue: (all born at Sterling, Illinois)
  i. Matilda, b. January 22, 1873
  ii. Henry "Harry" E., b. October 2, 1974
  iii. Abraham E., b. January 20, 1877
  iv. Frank E., b. January 19, 1879
  v. John E., b. May 12, 1882
  vi. Amos E., b. October 9, 1889

References:

Umble, John, *Descendants of Abraham Burkholder Ebersole and his Wife, Anna Ebersole Rutt*

64. ANNA R. EBERSOLE [Abraham B.[4], David M.[3], Jacob[2], Jacob[1]], daughter of Abraham B. and Anna E. (Rutt) Ebersole was born July 26, 1853, probably in Lancaster County, Pa. She died October 29, 1924 at Sterling, Illinois and is buried in the Science Ridge Cemetery at Sterling.

On October 11, 1898, Anna was married at Sterling, Illinois to John Leonard Reisner, a farmer and ordained Mennonite preacher. John Leonard was born October 11, 1853 at Chambersburg, Franklin County, Pa. He died August 23, 1892 at Sterling, Ill., and is buried at the Science Ridge Cemetery at Sterling.

John Leonard Reisner was a farmer and an ordained Mennonite preacher.

Issue: (all born at Sterling, Illinois)
  i. Lewis A., b. November 17, 1879
  ii. Mary Ellen, b. October 26, 1881
  iii. Naomi Esther, b. June 17, 1884
  iv. Charles Leonard, b. March 22, 1891
  v. Anna Catherine, b. May 10, 1894

References:

Umble, John, *Descendants of Abraham Burkholder Ebersole and his Wife, Anna Ebersole Rutt*

65. SABINA EBERSOLE [[Abraham B.[4], David M.[3], Jacob[2], Jacob[1]], daughter of Abraham B. and Anna E. (Rutt) Ebersole, was born December 22, 1855 in Lancaster County, Pa. She died April 4, 1934 and is buried in

the Violet Cemetery, Goshen, Indiana where she probably died.

On December 11, 1874, Sabina was married to Amos Stauffer Landis, a Mennonite farmer at Sterling, Illinois. Amos was born August 2, 1851 and died January 1, 1926. He, too, is buried at the Violet Cemetery at Goshen, Ind.

The Landis's were farmers and Mennonites.

Issue:

      i. Enos Clayton, b. February 11, 1876
     ii. Bessie Anna, b. September 12, 1878
   iii. Alice Maud, b. January 20, 1882
   iv. Lena May, b. September 18, 1883
    v. Austin E., b. November 18, 1885
   vi. Elwood E., b. May 13, 1889
  vii. Menno Claude, b. November 29, 1890
 viii. Mary Frances, b. April 11, 1892
   ix. Ruth Wion, b. June 14, 1893
    x. Florence Sabina, b. November 29, 1896
   xi. Esther Naomi, b. January 8, 1898

References:

Umble, John, *Descendants of Abraham Burkholder Ebersole and his Wife, Anna Ebersole Rutt*

66. MICHAEL RUTT EBERSOLE [Abraham B.[4], David M.[3], Jacob[2], Jacob[1]], son of Abraham B. and his wife, Anna E. (Rutt) Ebersole, was born June 15, 1858 near Elizabethtown, Lancaster County, Pa. He died August 1, 1924 at Souderton, Montgomery County, Pa. and is buried in the Mennonite Cemetery at Souderton, Pa.

On December 8, 1881, Michael was married to Annie Burkey Detweiler. Annie Was born July 20, 1855 in Montgomery County, Pa. She died December 9, 1940 at Souderton, Montgomery County, Pa. and is buried in the Mennonite Cemetery at Souderton.

Michael Ebersole and his family were Mennonites and farmers.

Issue:

   i. Jennie Detweiler, b. August 30, 1883
  ii. Eliza Mae, b. February 28, 1887; d. February 22, 1909 at Souderton, Montgomery County, Pa. Bur. in Souderton Mennonite Cemetery.

References:

Gospel Herald, March 6, 1909, p. 784, August 21, 1924, p. 431
Umble, John, *Descendants of Abraham Burkholder Ebersole and his
    Wife, Anna Ebersole Rutt*

    67. AMOS A. EBERSOLE [Abraham B.[4], David M.[3], Jacob[2], Jacob[1]], son of Abraham B. and his wife, Anna E. (Rutt) Ebersole, was born September 4, 1869 in Whiteside County, Illinois. His date and place of death are not now known.

    On June 30, 1897, Amos was married to Bertha Powers Thummel, a widow at Sterling, Illinois. She was born August 9, 1871 at St. Louis, Missouri. Her date and place of death are not presently known.

    Amos A. Ebersole was a homeopathic physician.

    Issue:
        i. Harold Leon, b. September 24, 1899; Harold married
           Charlotte Meador in 1932.
        ii. Raymond Arthur, April 27, 1901

    References:
Genealogical card catalog, Lancaster County Mennonite Historical
Society, Lancaster, Pa.
Umble, John, *Descendants of Abraham Burkholder Ebersole and his   Wife,
Anna Ebersole Rutt*

    68. DANIEL B. EBERSOLE [Samuel D.[4], David M.[3], Jacob[2], Jacob[1]], son of Samuel D. Ebersole and his wife,, the former Susannah Burkholder, was born October 5, 1863 in Lancaster County, Pa., probably near Elizabethtown. He died November 15, 1910 and is buried at the Mt. Tunnel Cemetery, Elizabethtown, Pa.

    Daniel was married to Laura Jane _____. Laura was born March 7, 1860. She died June 30, 1918 and is buried with her husband at the Mt. Tunnel Cemetery.

    Issue:
        i. Frank, b.
        ii. Stella Blanche, b. September 11, 1888; d. December 30,
           1896. Bur. Mt. Tunnel Cemetery with her parents.

    References:
Herald of Truth, February 1, 1897, p. 45
Inscriptions, Mt. Tunnel Cemetery, Elizabethtown, Pa.
Lancaster County, Pa. Orphans Court Records, Book O, Vol. 3, p. 329

Lancaster County, Pa. Wills, Will of Daniel B. Ebersole, Will Book T, Vol. 2, p. 506

Ibid., Will of Laura J. Ebersole, Will Book A., Vol. 3, p. 267

69. DAVID M. EBERSOLE [David B.[4], David M.[3], Jacob[2], Jacob[1]], son of David B. and Anna (Martin) Ebersole, was born September 3, 1866 in Lancaster County, Pa. He moved to Sterling, Illinois where he died on March 26, 1912. He is buried at the Science Ridge Cemetery at Sterling, Ill.

David was married to Hattie Frey, daughter of Henry B. Frey and his wife, the former Lizzie Kreider. Hattie was born February 3, 1867 and died February 11, 1926. She is buried with her husband at the Science Ridge Cemetery.

Issue:

    i. Roy Henry, b. February 26, 1892; d. November 11, 1967. Roy married November 26, 1914 to Ruth Nice. Ruth died November 19, 1933.

    ii. Lloyd who married Rhoda C. Long.

    iii. Bertha May, b. May 29, 1899; Bertha married David Conrad November 9, 1919.

    iv. Frank F., b. October 9, 1900;

    v. Milton M., b. January 6, 1906;

    vi. Amos, b.

    vii. Ann who married W. R. Souillard.

References:

Gospel Herald, December 12, 1967, p. 1122

Landis Book IV, pp. 150, 152

70. PETER C. EBERSOLE [Christian K.[4], Jacob M.[3], Jacob[2], Jacob[1]], son of Peter C. and Mary (Rutt) Ebersole, was born November 26, 1843, probably in Lancaster County, Pa. He died August 15, 1905 in Manheim Township, Lancaster County, Pa.

Peter C. Ebersole was married to Mary B. Eby.

Issue: (all born in Lancaster County, Pa.)

110.   i. Seth E., b. January 1, 1868

    ii. Anna E., b. October 5, 1869; d. October 5, 1869. Bur. Landisville Mennonite Cemetery, Landisville, Pa.

    iii. Susan E., b. August 18, 1875 in West Hempfield Township. Susan was married October 17, 1897 to

Phares Snavely. Phares was born in 1872 in Penn
Township, Lancaster County, Pa. .

      iv. Peter E., b.

References:

Brubacher, Jacob N., *The Brubacher Genealogy in America*, p. 24

Gerberich, Albert H., *Gravestone Inscriptions, Landisville Cemetery*

Gospel Herald, March 7, 1935, p. 1043

Lancaster County, Pa. Orphans Court, Marriage License Docket, Book Y,
      Vol. 1, p. 13578,, License No. 13578

Lancaster County, Pa. Orphans Court Records, Bond Book A, Vol. 3.
      p. 85

Mennonite Research Journal, Vol. 4, No. 1, p. 2

72. CHRISTIAN C. EBERSOLE [Christian K.[4], Jacob M.[3], Jacob[2],
Jacob[1]], son of Christian K. and Mary (Rutt) Ebersole, was born July 2, 1850
in Lancaster County, Pa. He died October 30, 1910 in Conoy Township,
Lancaster County, Pa. He is buried at Good's Mennonite Cemetery.

    On December 22, 1874, Christian was married to Mary M. Ebersole who
was born December 14, 1848. She died April 10, 1926 and is buried at
Good's Mennonite Cemetery with her husband.

    Christian C. Ebersole was ordained a deacon in the Mennonite Church on
March 21, 1901.

      Issue: (all born in Lancaster County, Pa.)

        i. David E., b. January 12, 1884

        ii. Martha, b. January 31, 1880 in Conoy Township. She
           died January 23, 1945. Martha Ebersole was married
           twice. Her first husband, whom she married on January
           11, 1921, was John W. Fry who was born in 1876.
           John was born in Newberry Township, York County, Pa.
           Her second husband was Amos R. Ebersole whom she
           married October 18, 1927 at Deodate, Dauphin County,
           Pa.

    References:

Diary of Preacher Jacob N. Brubacher

Albert H., *Gravestone Inscriptions, Good' Mennonite Meeting
    House*

Gospel Herald, December 15, 1910

Inscriptions, Good's Mennonite Cemetery, near Elizabethtown, Pa.

Lancaster County, Pa., Orphans Court, Marriage, License Docket Book U,
    Vol. 4, License No. 10770
Ibid., Book N, Vol. 5, License No. 6890
Lancaster County, Pa. Orphans Court Records, Bond Book F, Vol. 3,
    p. 257
The Lancaster Intelligencer, Lancaster, Pa., December 30, 1874

72. DAVID C. EBERSOLE [Christian K.[4], Jacob M.[3], Jacob[2], Jacob[1]],
son of Christian K. and Mary (Rutt) Ebersole, was born January 15, 1857 in
Lancaster County, Pa. He died April 17, 1933 and is buried in the Kraybill
Mennonite Cemetery, near Mt. Joy, Lancaster County, Pa.
    David was married to Katherine B. Heistand on November 6, 1881.
Katherine was born November 21, 1859. She died August 13, 1932 and is
buried with her husband at the Kraybill Mennonite Cemetery.
    Issue:
        i. Abraham H., b. April 4, 1885; d. June 28, 1906. Bur.
           Kraybill Mennonite Cemetery.
       ii. Fanny H., b. December 13, 1887; d. August 10, 1957
           unmarried. Bur. Kraybill Mennonite Cemetery.
      iii. Mary H., b. May 31, 1892; d. May 3, 1953 unmarried.
           Bur. Kraybill Mennonite Cemetery.
       iv. Rebecca H., b. July 7, 1896
        v. David H., b. September 17, 1889
       vi. Martin H., b. September 15, 1882
      vii. Clayton H., b. March 27, 1901
     viii. Amos H., b. September 11, 1902
    References:
Gerberich, Albert H., *Gravestone Inscriptions, Kraybill Cemetery*
Herald of Truth, July 12, 1906, p. 259
Inscriptions, Kraybill Cemetery, near Mt. Joy, Pa.
Lancaster County, Pa. Orphans Court Records, Bond Book U, Vol. 3,
    p. 29
Lancaster County, Pa. Records of Births
Lancaster County, Pa. Wills, Will of Fanny H. Ebersole, Will Book G,
    Vol. 4, p. 386
Mennonite Research Journal, Lancaster, Pa., Vol. III, No. 3, p. 36

73. JOSEPH N. EBERSOLE [Joseph[4], Jacob G.[3], Christian[2], Jacob[1]],

son of Joseph N. and Anna (Nissley) Ebersole on June 8, 1843 in Lancaster County, Pa. He died October 14, 1867 in East Donegal Township (Springville), Lancaster County, Pa.

Joseph was married to Catharine _____.

Issue:

        i. Lavina who married a man whose surname was Peters..

References:

Daily Express, October 15, 1867

Herald of Truth, November 1867, p. 176

Lancaster Count, Pa. Deeds, Deed Book E, Vol. 14, pp. 544, 547

Ibid., Book D, Vol. 13, p. 271

Lancaster County, Pa. Orphans Court Records, Book X, Vol. 1, p. 61

Ibid., Miscellaneous Book 1867 - 1870, pp. 40, 198, 199

  "   Miscellaneous Book 1882 - 1883, pp. 612, 613

Lancaster County, Pa. Wills, Will of Anna Ebersole, Will Book L,
     Vol. 2, p. 299

73. ELI D. EBERSOLE [Solomon R.[4], Jacob G.[3], Christian[2], Jacob[1]], son of Solomon R. and Sarah E. (Diffenderfer) Ebersole, was born March 7, 1860 in Lancaster County, Pa. He died at Mt. Joy, Lancaster County, Pa.

Eli married twice. His first wife, whose name is not now known, died June 23, 1925. His second wife was Minnie Dietz who he married on July 26, 1926 at Mt. Joy, Lancaster County, Pa.

    Issue: (both born in Lancaster County, Pa.)

        i. Margaret S., b. 1885 in Rapho Township. Margaret
           married Elvin E. Baker on June 22, 1902. Elvin was born
           in 1860 at Dillsburg, York County, Pa.

        ii. Walter S., b.

References:

Lancaster County, Pa. Orphans Court, Marriage License Docket, Book
     K, Vol. 5, License No. 5145

Ibid., Book K, Vol. 2, License No. 19379

Lancaster County, Pa. Orphans Court Records, Bond Book Y, Vol. 3,
     p. 27

74. SOLOMON D. EBERSOLE [Solomon R.[4], Jacob G.[3], Christian[2], Jacob[1]], son of Solomon R. and Sarah E. (Diffenderfer) Ebersole, was born February 18, 1868 in Mt. Joy, Lancaster County, Pa. He died in 1941 and is

buried at the Lancaster Cemetery, Lancaster, Pa.

On November 9, 1893, Solomon was married to Grace B. Eberly at Lancaster, Pa. Grace was born about 1873 at Manheim, Lancaster County, Pa. She died December 14, 1928 and is buried at the Lancaster Cemetery with her husband.

Issue: (all born in Lancaster County, Pa.)

    i. Gertrude M., b. about 1898 at Lancaster, Pa.

    ii. S. Earl, b. about 1899

    iii. Edith I., b. 1895. Edith was married to Lloyd J. Rhoads on November 28, 1935 at Lancaster, Pa. Lloyd, son of W. S. Rhoads, was born about 1906 at Lancaster, Lancaster County,Pa.

    iv. Myrtle V., b. about 1902. Myrtle was married November 28, 1835 to Earl W. Rhoads at Lancaster, Pa. Earl was born about the year 1908 in Manor Township, Lancaster County, Pa.

    v. Mabel E., b. 1904; d. 1905. Bur. Lancaster Cemetery.

    vi. Gertrude who married Paul Zimmerman on December 17, 1928. Paul was born about 1903 in Eden Township, Lancaster County, Pa..

References:

Lancaster County, Pa. Orphans Court, Marriage License Docket, Marriages, Book O, Vol. 5, License No. 7145

Ibid., Book J, Vol. 6, License No. 17679

   "   Book J, Vol. 6, License No. 17679

   "   Book P, License No. 9055

   "   Book K, Vol. 6, License No. 18048

Rineer, A. Hunter, *Lancaster County Cemetery Inscriptions*, Vol. 27, Lancaster Cemetery, p. 278

75. AMOS D. EBERSOLE [Solomon R.[4], Jacob G.[3], Christian[2], Jacob[1]], son of Solomon R. and Sarah E. (Diffenderfer) Ebersole, was born June 28, 1870 at Columbia, Lancaster County, Pa. He died October 29, 1917 at Lancaster, Pa.

On December 23, 1894, Amos was married to Elizabeth M. Rutter, daughter of Samuel S. Rutter, at Lancaster, Pa. Elizabeth was born in Eden, Manheim Township, Lancaster County, Pa. She died March 4, 1959.

issue: (all born in Lancaster County, Pa.)

i .Helen M., b. 1896 at Lancaster; She was married
September 6, 1916 to Raymond F. Bone at Lancaster,
Pa.
ii. Ethel A., b. about 1898 at Lancaster; Ethel was married
March 22, 1919 to Lloyd H. Kennedy.
iii. Charles, b. September 2, 1899
iv. Milton R., b.

References:
Lancaster County, Pa. Orphans Court, Marriage License Docket, Book S,,
License No. 10426
Ibid., Book H, Vol. 4, License No. 4143
" Book O, Vol. 4, License No. 7763
Lancaster County, Pa. Wills, Will of Amos D. Ebersole, Will Book Z,
Vol. 2, p. 483
Ibid., Will of Elizabeth Ebersole, Will Book I, Vol. 4, p. 247

76. JOHN D. EBERSOLE [Solomon R.[4], Jacob G.[3], Christian[2],
Jacob[1]], son of Solomon D. and Sarah (Diffenderfer) Ebersole, was born in
1889 in Manheim Township, Lancaster County, Pa. He died January 21,
1978 in Manheim Township, Lancaster County, Pa.
On March 17, 1907, John was married to Mattie Benedict Irvin at
Lancaster, Pa. Mattie was born in 1886 at New Danville, Lancaster County,
Pa. She died April 22, 1947.
Issue: (all born at Lancaster, Lancaster County, Pa.)
i. Harold I., b. 1908
ii. Irvin, b.
iii. Alma, b. 1928; Alma was married February 14, 1940 to
Ray G. Rice. Ray was born in 1911 at Coatesville,
Chester County, Pa.

References:
Lancaster County, Pa. Orphans Court, Marriage License Docket, Book
V, Vol. 6, License No. 23897
Ibid., Book N, Vol. 3, License No. 2234
" Book O, Vol. 6, License No. 20391
Lancaster County, Pa. Wills, Will of John D. Ebersole, File No. 155

77. Jacob R. Ebersole, [John R.[4], Jacob G.[3], Christian[2], Jacob[1]], son of
John R. and Annie (Rutt) Ebersole, was born January 13, 1851 and died

April 10, 1904.

Jacob was married to Sarah Ebersole, the daughter of Jacob K. and Anna Ebersole, at Sterling, Illinois. Sarah was born July 18, 1850 and died January 6, 1940.

Issue:
        i. Edwin, b.
        ii. Roy, b.
        iii. Noah, b.
        iv. Reuben, b.
        v. Anna, b.

References:
Gospel Herald, January 25, 1940, p. 927

78. MARY EBERSOLE [Peter R.[4], Peter R.[3], Christian[2], Jacob[1]], daughter of Peter R. and Susan (Kendig) Ebersole, was born in February of 1846 in Conoy Township, Lancaster County, Pa. She died March 10, 1901.

On August 27, 1867, Mary was married to Cyrus Oldweiler at Elizabethtown, Pa. Cyrus, son of Philip Oldweiler and Susan Barnhard, was born August 27, 1840. His date and place of death are not known.

Issue:
        i. Amanda who married Isaac Engle.
        ii. Isaiah who married Fanny Landis.
        iii. Oliver
        iv. Albert
        v. Clayton
        vi. William
        vii. Harry

References:
Beers, J. H. Co., *Biographical Annals of Lancaster County, Pa.*, p.   1361
Records of Christ Evangelical Lutheran Church, Elizabethtown, Pa.
    translated and transcribed by Frederick S. Weiser, p. 339

79. MARTIN K. EBERSOLE [Peter R.[4], Peter R.[3], Christian[2], Jacob[1]], son of Peter R. and Susan (Kendig) Ebersole, was born in 1853 in Conoy Township, Lancaster County, Pa. He died April 25, 1899 in Conoy Township, Lancaster County, Pa. and is buried at Good's Mennonite Cemetery, near Elizabethtown, Pa.

Martin was married to Amanda Ebersole on November 14, 1871 at

Elizabethtown, Pa. Amanda was born in 1852 in West Donegal Township, Lancaster County, Pa. She died April 2, 1914 and is buried at Good's Mennonite Cemetery with her husband.

Issue:

i. Emma, b. 1872. Emma married June 2, 1892 to Joseph L. Smith at Elizabethtown, Pa. He was born in 1872 in Conoy Township, Lancaster County, Pa.

ii. Harvey E., b. October 11, 1875; d. February 27, 1973

iii. John M., b. 1881

iv. Barbara A., b. 1882. Barbara married February 18, 1902 to John C. Greenly at Elizabethtown, Pa. John was born in 1879 at Maytown, Lancaster County, Pa.

v. Samuel M., b. November 25, 1885

vi. Susie E., b. 1887 at Bainbridge, Lancaster County, Pa. On March 12, 1905 Susie was married to John H. Groff, a farm laborer. John was born in 1882 in Providence Township, Lancaster County, Pa.

vii. Mabel Irene, b. 1888 at Mt. Joy; She was married June 11, 1905 to Henry M. Forry, a farmer. Henry was born in 1882 in West Hempfield Township, Lancaster County, Pa.

viii. Mary E., b. 1890 at Palmyra, Lebanon County, Pa. Mary was married May 13, 1926 to Christian Zook at Deodate, Dauphin County, Pa. He was born in 1899 in Salisbury Township, Lancaster County, Pa.

References:

Gerberich, Albert H., *Gravestone Inscriptions, Good's Mennonite Meeting House, West Donegal Township*

Inscriptions, Good's Mennonite Cemetery, near Elizabethtown, Pa.

Records of Christ Evangelical Lutheran Church, Elizabethtown, Pa. translated and transcribed by Frederick S. Weiser, p. 342

Lancaster County, Pa. Orphans Court, Marriage License Docket, Book M, License No. 7387

Ibid., Book C, Vol. 3, License No. 11211

" Book B. Vol. 3, License No. 981

" License No. 18944

" Book J, Vol. 5, License No. 4866

Lancaster County, Pa. Orphans Court Records, Bond Book S.

80. PETER K. EBERSOLE [Peter R.[4], Peter R.[3], Christian[2], Jacob[1]], son of Peter R. and Susan (Kendig), Ebersole was born April 1, 1853 in Lancaster County, Pa. He died August 2, 1916 in Mt. Joy Township, Lancaster County, Pa. and is buried in the "Ebersole burying ground."

On August 17, 1871, Peter was married to Barbara I. _____ . Barbara was born August 20, 1853. She died January 27, 1916 and is buried with her husband in the "Ebersole burying ground."

Issue: (all born in Lancaster County, Pa.)
- i. Harry D., b. 1877 in Conoy Township
- ii. Annie, b. 1879 in Conoy Township. Annie was married to Monroe King on June 18, 1896 at Elizabethtown, Pa. Monroe was born in 1874 in Lower Swatara Township, Dauphin County, Pa.
- iii. Sadie D., b. December 1, 1884 at Elizabethtown. Sadie was married July 2, 1904 to Harvey Hoffer Martin.

References:
Gerberich, Albert H., *Gravestone Inscriptions, Ebersole Burying Ground*, p. 202
Lancaster County, Pa. Orphans Court, Marriage License Docket, Book V, License No. 12112
Lancaster County, Pa. Wills, Will of P. K. Ebersole, Will Book Z, Vol. 2, p. 131
Records of Christ Evangelical Lutheran Church, Elizabethtown, Pa., translated and transcribed by Frederick S. Weiser
Retherford, Audrey L., *Cemetery Records of Conoy Township (Lancaster County, Pa.) Family Graveyards,* 1979, p. 8

81 AMANDA K. EBERSOLE [Peter R.[4], Peter R.[3], Christian[2], Jacob[1]], daughter of Peter R. and Susan (Kendig) Ebersole, was born May 9, 1863.

Amanda was married October 2, 1864 to Frank Landis, son of John Frick Landis and Magdalene G. (Keller) Landis.

Issue:
- i. Katie E., b. June 18, 1885; d. unmarried November 19, 1906.
- ii. Clayton, b. July 16, 1886; d. March 16, 1965. Clayton

married Alice E. Miller, b. February 27, 1883;
d. February 10, 1965.

  iii. John E., b. June 28, 1889; John married Ellen Weidner,
b. May 5, 1888; d. December 6, 1969.

  iv. Paris E., b. November 29, 1892; d. February 8, 1901.

   v. Mary E., b. July 20, 1894; d. June 13, 1956. Mary
married Phares N. Frank, b. October 5, 1881; d. August
13, 1944.

  vi. Walter E., b. September 15, 1895; d. February 5,1901.

  vii. Paul E., b. September 26, 1898

  viii. Chester E., b. November 25, 1900

  ix. Anna E., b. October 24, 1903. m. Paul Zeager,
b. August 15, 1895; d. November 10, 1965.

   x. Grace E., b. October 16, 1905. Grace married Clyde H.
Lamp, b. May 2, ____.

  xi. Mabel E., b. September 11, 1907. Mabel was married to
Joseph J. Wert, b. February 23, 1908.

  xii. Ruth E., b. January 9, 1910. Ruth was married Clayton
M. Hess, b. May 10, 1906.

References:
Landis, Frank K., Family bible owned by Mrs. Anna E. Zeager

82. ELIZABETH EBERSOLE [Peter R.[4], Peter R.[3], Christian[2],
Jacob[1]], daughter of Peter R. and Susan (Kendig) Ebersole, is little known.
She was deceased before 1903.

Elizabeth was married to Christian W. Oberholtzer.

Issue:

   i. Isaiah Ebersole, b. May 11, 1883; d. July 29, 1956.
Isaiah was a minister but the denomination is unknown.

References:
Beers, J. H. Co., *Biographical Annals of Lancaster County, Pa.*, p.   1361
Pennsylvania Mennonite Heritage, Vol. 1, No. 2, p. 2

83. PETER L. EBERSOLE [Jacob R.[4], Peter R.[3], Christian[2], Jacob[1]],
son of Jacob R. and Anna R. (Lehman) Ebersole, was born in 1856 in
Lancaster County, Pa. He died in 1921.

On October 27, 1872, he was married to Anna M. Snyder at Lancaster,
Pa.

Peter was ordained a Mennonite preacher on December 31, 1903

    Issue: (all born in Conoy Township, Lancaster County, Pa.)

         i. Elmer S., b. 1879

        ii. John S., b. 1882

      iii. Lizzie S., b. June 11, 1885; d. October 4, 1885. Bur. Ebersole Cemetery.

      iv. Ella S., b. 1886; Ella was married December 24, 1914 to Norman E. Lehigh at Mountville, Lancaster County, Pa.. He was the son of Abraham and Sarah Lehigh.

       v. Ida S., b. April 25, 1888; d. September 4, 1888. Bur. Ebersole Cemetery.

      vi. Jacob S., b. 1889

References:

Lancaster County, Pa. Orphans Court, Marriage License Docket, Book C, Vol. 4, License No. 1794

Retherford, Audrey L., *Cemetery Records of Conoy Township (Lancaster County, Pa.), Family Graveyards*, 1979, p. 8

Weaver, Martin G., *Mennonites of the Lancaster Conference*, p. 99

    84. JACOB L. EBERSOLE [Jacob R.[4], Peter R.[3], Christian[2], Jacob[1]], son of Jacob R. and Anna R. (Lehman) Ebersole, was born May 3, 1866 in Conoy Township, Lancaster County, Pa. He died December 2, 1945 and is buried in the "Ebersole Burying Ground."

On October 13, 1888, Jacob was married to Sara (also Sadie) Ober at Manheim, Lancaster County, Pa. Sara, the daughter of John Ober, was born February 21, 1865 in West Donegal Township, Lancaster County, Pa. She died July 9, 1924 and is buried with her husband in the "Ebersole Burying Ground."

After the death of Sara, Jacob was married a second time on March 21, 1926 to Alice Brandt, daughter of Joseph and Elizabeth (Dysinger) Shank.

Jacob L. Ebersole was a farmer.

    Issue: (all born in Conoy Township, Lancaster County, Pa.)

         i. Johnson O., b. 1889

        ii. Jennie O., b. 1891; Jennie was married January 16, 1913 to Frank H. Weaber at Elizabethtown, Pa. Frank was born about 1889 in West Donegal Township, Lancaster County, Pa.

      iii. Reuben O., b. 1892

iv. Bertha O., b. March 8, 1894; m. June 30, 1917 to Christian Wittle at Elizabethtown, Pa. Christian, son of Cyrus and Kate (Diffenderfer) Wittle was born in Lancaster County, Pa. Lancaster County, Pa Record of Births records her name as Birtha and her place of birth Elizabeth Township.

v. Elizabeth (also Lizzie) O., b. February 25, 1895; Elizabeth was married April 8, 1917 to Tillman Ebersole, son of Levi Landis Ebersole and Anna E. Miller, at Elizabethtown, Pa.

vi. Agnes O., b. 1896. Agnes married October 20, 1921 to Harvey Y. Weaver at Lancaster, Pa. Harvey, son of E. S. Weaver and Mary Young, was born in 1897 in East Donegal Township, Lancaster County, Pa.

vii. Sara (also Sadie) O., b. 1897; Sara married September 29, 1918 to Norman H. Shank at Penbrook, Dauphin County, Pa. Norman, son of Michael S. Shank, was born in 1897 in Lancaster County, Pa.

viii. Emma O., b. 1899; Emma married May 7, 1925 to J. Ira Heisey at Shiremanstown, Cumberland County, Pa. Ira, son of Samuel L. and Lizzie (Gibble) Heisey, was born in 1899 in Mt. Joy Township, Lancaster County, Pa.

ix. Anna M., b.

x. Jacob R., b. June 10, 1905; Jacob M December 18, 1930 to Ruth A. Winters at Lancaster, Pa. Ruth, daughter of Abram and Louise (Alwein) Winters, was born in 1909 in Mt. Joy Township, Lancaster County, Pa.

References:

Beers, J. H. Co., *Biographical Annals of Lancaster County, Pa.*, p.   861
Lancaster County, Pa. Orphans Court, Marriage License Docket, Marriages, Book P, Vol. 3, License No. 7909
Ibid., Book J, Vol. 4, License No. 5383
  "   Book J, Vol. 4, License No. 5102
  "   Book V, Vol. 4, License No. 11528
  "   Book N, Vol. 4, License No. 7191
  "   Book G, Vol. 5, License No. 3416

"   Book W, Vol. 5, License No. 11072
"   Book E, License No. 3196
"   Book J, Vol. 5, License No. 4679
Lancaster County, Pa. Record of Births
Lancaster Intelligencer Journal, Lancaster, Pa., July 24, 1985
Lebanon County, Pa. Orphans Court, Marriage License Docket, Vol. 26,
    p. 40

85. HENRY H. EBERSOLE [John F.[4], Christian R.[3], Christian[2], Jacob[1]], son of John F. and Nancy (Horst) Ebersole, was born in 1842 in Franklin County, Pa. He died September 28, 1921 at Clarence Center, New York and is buried in the Clarence Center Cemetery.

Henry was married to Nancy Rhodes. Nancy, daughter of John and Anna (Martin) Rhodes, was born August 6, 1840 in Franklin County, Pa. She died February 27, 1910 at Clarence Center, New York where she is buried.

    Issue:

        i. John K.
        ii. Emma
        iii. Leah
        iv. Amanda E.
        v. Aaron
        vi. Lyman
        vii. Reuben
        viii. Anna

    References:

Samuel S. Wenger, Editor-in-Chief, *The Wenger Book, A Foundation Book of American Wengers*, p. 643

86. CHRISTIAN H. EBERSOLE [John F.[4], Christian R.[3], Christian[2], Jacob[1]], son of John F. and Nancy (Horst) Ebersole, was born November 11, 1843 in Franklin County, Pa. He died February 5, 1912 at Strasburg, Virginia where he is buried.

Christian married but his wife's name is unknown.

    Issue:

        i. A daughter who married P. C. Petery
        ii. George

    References:

Samuel S. Wenger, Editor-in-chief, *The Wenger Book, A Foundation Book of*

87. LEVI D. EBERSOLE [John F.[4], Christian R.[3], Christian[2], Jacob[1]], son of John F. and Nancy (Horst) Ebersole, was born May 3, 1846 at Chambersburg, Franklin County, Pa. He died March 6, 1920 at North Tonawanda, New York.

Levi was married but his wife's name is not now known.

Issue:

       i. Ruth
      ii. Fannie
    iii. J. Frank

References:

Samuel S. Wenger, Editor-in-chief, *The Wenger Book, A Foundation Book of American Wengers,* p. 643

88. SAMUEL E. EBERSOLE[Daniel[4], Jacob[3], Martin[2], Jacob[1]], son of Daniel Ebersole and Elizabeth Ebersole, was born February 12, 1847 in Mt. Joy Township, Lancaster County, Pa. He died October 24, 1934 in Conoy Township, Lancaster County and is buried at Good's Mennonite Cemetery, near Elizabethtown, Pa.

Samuel was married to Mary Sandoe in October of 1873. Mary, daughter of Henry and Elizabeth (Stibgeon) Sandoe, was born October 23, 1849 in East Donegal Township, Lancaster County, Pa. She died 21 March 1928 and is buried at Good's Mennonite Cemetery with her husband.

Samuel was a Mennonite, his wife belonged to Zion's Children.

Issue: (all born in Lancaster County, Pa.)

       i. Ida S., b. 1875; d. 30 January 1882. Bur. Good's Mennonite Cemetery.
      ii. Alice S. (twin), b. 1876 in Conoy Township
    iii. Albert S. (twin), b. 1876 in Conoy Township
    iv. Raymond S., b. 15 October 1879
     v. Grace S., b. 8 February 1888

References:

Beers, J. H. & Co., *Biographical Annals of Lancaster County, Pennsylvania,* . 1362

Gerberich, Albert H., *Gravestone Inscriptions, Good's Mennonite Meeting House*

Inscriptions, Good's Mennonite Cemetery, Elizabethtown, Pa.

Kauffman, Charles F., *A Genealogy and History of the Kauffman-Coffman*
    Families of North America, p. 347
Lancaster County, Pa. Wills, Will of Samuel E. Ebersole, Will Book N,
    Vol. 3, p. 132

89. AMOS E. EBERSOLE [Daniel[4], Jacob[3], Martin[2], Jacob[1]], son of
Daniel Ebersole and Elizabeth Ebersole, was born November 20, 1848 in
Lancaster County, Pa. The *Herald of Truth* records his date of birth as
November 20 1849. He died January 15, 1874 in Conoy Township, Lancaster
County, Pa.
    On September 25, 1869, Amos was married to Elizabeth Risser.
    Issue: (both born in Lancaster County, Pa.)
            i. Ellen, b.
            ii. Ada, b.
    Both Ellen and Ada were under the age of 14 years in January of 1876.
Ada was still a minor in the year 1882.
    References:
Herald of Truth, May 1874, p. 94
Lancaster County, Pa. Deeds, Book B, Vol. 12, p. 319
Lancaster County, Pa. Orphans Court Records, Accounts and Reports,
    Book 31, p. 248
Ibid., Book 56, p. 160
Lancaster County, Pa. Orphans Court Records, Miscellaneous Book
    1873-1875, pp. 167, 259, 658
Ibid., 1875-1876, pp. 258, 436

90. ABRAHAM E. EBERSOLE [Daniel[4], Jacob[3], Martin[2], Jacob[1]], son
of Daniel Ebersole and Elizabeth Ebersole was born November 16, 1858 in
Lancaster County, Pa. He died February 13, 1914 and is buried at Good's
Mennonite Cemetery, near Elizabethtown, Pa.
    Abraham was married twice. His first wife was Mary Anna Gish who was
born February 5, 1859. She died March 13, 1879 and is buried at Good's
Mennonite Cemetery.
    Issue: (all born in Lebanon County, Pa.)
            i. Minerva G., b. 22 February 1879 at Annville
After the death of his first wife, Abraham married a second time to Sarah
C. Westenberger, daughter of David and Sarah (Gosser) Westenberger.

Sarah was born 3 June 1852. She died 20 September 1911 and is buried at Good's Mennonite Cemetery, near Elizabethtown, Pa..

Issue:

   ii. Ellen W., b. 19 January 1882
   iii. David W., b. 1886
   iv. Sally W., b. 26 January 1889
   v. Katie W., b. 1896

References:

Beers, J. H. Co., *Biographical Annals of Lancaster County, Pennsylvania,* pp. 83, 1362

Gerberich, Albert H., *Gravestone Inscriptions, Good's Mennonite Meeting*
  House

Lancaster County, Pa. Orphans Court Records, Book J, Vol. 3, p. 103

Lebanon County, Pa. Orphans Court, Marriage License Docket, Vol. 18, p. 488

  91. JACOB E. EBERSOLE [Daniel[4], Jacob[3], Martin[2], Jacob[1]], son of Daniel and Elizabeth Ebersole, was born October 9, 1861 in Lancaster County, Pa. He died January 29, 1939 at Heilmandale, Lebanon County, Pa. and is buried at Dohner's Mennonite Meeting House which is located in North Annville Township, near the Union Water Works, in Lebanon County, Pa..

  On October 24, 1882, Jacob was married to Kate Gingrich. Kate, the daughter of Joseph K. and Elizabeth (Reist) Gingrich, was born September 8, 1864. She died January 22, 1912 and is buried with her husband at Dohner's Mennonite Meeting House.

  After the death of Kate, Jacob was married to Annie Kreider, a widow and daughter of Moses and Sarah (Bomberger) Kreider. Annie's first husband was Moses K. Kreider. Annie was born November 1, 1878. She died October 5, 1941 at Wernersville, Berks County, Pa. Annie is buried at Gingrich's Mennonite Cemetery, North Cornwall Township, Lebanon County, Pa.

  Jacob was a farmer and was also an ordained Mennonite preacher having been ordained 15 September 1904.

  Issue: (all born in Lebanon County, Pa.)

111.   i. Cora Gingrich b. September 28, 1883
112.   ii. Irvin Gingrich, b. June 20, 1885

113.	iii.	Ammon Gingrich, b. April 7, 1887.
114.	iv.	Elizabeth Gingrich, February 22, 1889.
115.	v.	Clayton Gingrich, b. September 26, 1890 at Annville

vi. Jacob G., b. January 17, 1893 in North Annville Township, Lebanon County, Pa. He died June 12, 1894 and is buried at Dohner's Mennonite Cemetery in North Annville Township, Lebanon County, Pa.

116. vii. Edna Mae, b. February 19, 1894 in North Annville Township

viii. Martin A., b. March 20, 1895 in North Annville Township. He died April 3, 1895 and is buried at Dohner's Mennonite Cemetery, North Annville Township, Lebanon County, Pa.

ix. Della Catharine, b. November 5, 1899 at Myersville, Pa. She died May 6, 1900 and is buried at Dohner's Mennonite Cemetery in North Annville Township

x. Viola Esther, b. June 22, 1906 at Myersville; d. June 22, 1906 and is buried at Dohner's Mennonite Cemetery, in North Annville Township, Lebanon County, Pa.

Reference:

Francis, J. G. *History of the Kreider Family from the Pen of Rev. J. G. Francis,* Lebanon Daily News, Lebanon, Pa., June 5, 1919

Gordon, John D., Correspondence

Inscriptions, Cemetery of Dohner's Mennonite Meeting House

Lebanon County Pa., Coroner's Records

Lebanon County, Pa. , Orphans Court, Marriage License Docket, Vol. 25, p. 37

Ibid. Vol. 18, p. 469

Lebanon County, Pa., Register of Births

Lebanon County, Pa., Register of Deaths

Ibid. Will of Annie Ebersole, Will Book O, p.444

Lebanon County, Pa., Wills, Will of Jacob E. Ebersole, Will Book P, p. 628

Lebanon Courier, Lebanon, Pa., October 30, 1908, November 1, 1882

Lebanon Daily News, Lebanon, Pa., January 30, 1939, October 6, 1941

Mennonite Research Journal, Lancaster, Pa., Vol. V, No. 1

Records of Christ Reformed Church, Annville, Pa.

The Annville, Gazette, Annville, Pa., October 28, 2883

The Annville Journal, Annville, Pa.,March 25, 1905

92. JOHN A. WITMEYER [Elizabeth A.[5], John M.[4]. Jacob B.[3], John[2],

Jacob[1]], son of Adam ,H. and Elizabeth A. (Ebersole) Witmeyer, was born October 16, 1860 in Lebanon County, Pa. His date and place of death are not now known.

In 1884, John was married to Sallie Snoke by the Rev. J. H. Deitzler.. John and Sallie were the parents of 8 children.

Issue:

i. Cyrus B., b. September 4, 1891; d. April 19, 1895

The remaining children whose names are not known survived the many dangers of childhood in the 19th century and all grew to become adults.

References:

Witmeyer, John A., *History of the Witmeyer Family*

93. HENRY CLINTON LONGENECKER EBERSOLE [Elias A.[5], John[4], Jacob.[3], John[2], Jacob[1]], son of Elias A. and Catharine (Longenecker) Ebersole, was born September 1, 1866 in Londonderry Township, Lebanon County, Pa. He died December 22, 1934 at Lebanon, Lebanon County, Pa. and is buried in the cemetery adjoining the Salem Reformed church, Campbelltown, Lebanon County, Pa.

Clinton (the name by which he was best known) was married to Fannie Knoll Shanamn on December 12, 1891 at Jonestown, Lebanon County, Pa. Fannie, the daughter of Samuel and Frany (Knoll) Shanaman was born August 20, 1872 in North Annville Township, Lebanon County, Pa. She died in childbirth on December 31,1893 and is buried in the churchyard of the United Zion Children, Annville, Pa.

Issue:

117.   i. Franny (or Frany) Irene, b. January 1, 1893

After the death of his wife, Fannie, Clinton was married to Clara Alice Maulfair on April 25,1895 at Annville, Lebanon County, Pa. Clara, daughter of Elijah and Louisa Maulfair, was born November 2, 1866 in Lebanon County, Pa., probably at Palmyra. He died May 25, 1931 at Lebanon, Pa. and is buried with her husband at the Salem Reformed Church Cemetery, Campbelltown, Pa.

Clinton (the name by which he was best known) was a farm implement dealer at 308 N. Railroad Street, Palmyra, Pa. This business was ended by a disastrous fire in the early nineteen-twenties. He subsequently became a carpenter and builder.

References:

Ebersole, Clinton, Family bible

Gerberich, Albert H., *Gravestone Inscriptions, United Christian children Cemetery, North Annville, Pa.*
Inscriptions, Salem reformed Church Cemetery, Campbelltown, Pa.
Lebanon County, Pa., Orphans Court, Marriage License Docket, Vol. 5, P. 362
Ibid., Vol. 7, p. 593
Records of Christ Reformed Church, Annville, Pa.

94. ALLEN LONGENECKER EBERSOLE [Elias A.[5], John[4], Jacob.[3], John[2], Jacob[1]], son of Elias A. and Catharine (Longenecker)Ebersole, was born February 5, 1868 in Londnnderry Township, Lebanon County, Pa. He died August 12, 1929 at Palmyra, Lebanon County, Pa. and is buried in the Spring Creek Cemetery, Hershey, Dauphin County, Pa.

Allen was married to Minerva Elizabeth Mutch on August 6, 1892.. Minerva, the daughter of Henry and Sallie Mutch, was born October 3,1868. She died June 24, 1950 and is buried with her husband in the Spring Creek Cemetery.

Allen Ebersole was a ;lifelong carpenter. He and his family resided in Palmyra where they were members of the Palmyra Church of the Brethren.

Issue: (all born in Lebanon County, Pa.)

118.   i. Ella M., b. September 16, 1893

                     ii. John Herman, b. August 3, 1899. On February 13, 1932 John H. Ebersole was married to Ila Ruth Preston at Palmyra, Pa. Ila was born March 8, 1904, the daughter of Homas J. and Urada (Walker) Preston. She died February 8, 1934 and is buried in the Spring Creek Cemetery, Hershey, Pa.

119.   iii. Harry M., b. August 10, 1902

References:

Carper, F. S., *History of the Palmyra Church of the Brethren 1892-1967*, p. 307, Printed by Forry and Hacker, Lancaster, Pa.
Coroner's Report, Lebanon County, Pa.
Gravestone Inscriptions, Spring Creek Cemetery, Hershey, Pa.
Lebanon County, Pa.,, Orphans Court, Marriage License Docket, Vol. 6, p.3
Ibid., Vol. 36, p. 715
   "   Vol. 52, p. 85
Lebanon County, Pa., Report of Births

Lebanon County, Pa., Wills, Will of Allen L. Ebersole, Book N, p. 224

95. EMMA LONGENECKER EBERSOLE [Elias A.[5], John[4], Jacob.[3], John[2], Jacob[1]], daughter of Elias A. and Catharine (Longenecker) Ebersole, was born September 1,1869 in Londonderry Township, Lebanon County, Pa. She died March 12, 1945 and is buried in the Hershey Cemetery, Hershey, Dauphin County, Pa.

On July 23, 1892, Emma was married to Clayton Forry at Lebanon County, Pa. Clayton was born in Berks County, Pa., the son of Jonathan and Mary Forry.

Clayton was a hostler.

Issue:

| 120. | i. Paul J.,b. April 28,1892 |
| 121. | ii. Magdalena A. b., 1893 |

Emma and Clayton were divorced by the Lebanon County Courts April, 9, 1896. After the divorce, Emma was married to John Franklin Batdorf. John was born July 18, 1855. He died September 10, 1935 and is buried at the Spring Creek Cemetery, Hershey, Pa.

The Batdorf family lived at Palmyra, Pa.

References:
Batdorf, Virginia Faust, *The Batdorf Family History*, 1990, pp. 84, 85
Carper, F. S., *History of the Palmyra Church of the Brethren 1892-1967*,
    Printed by Forry and Hacker, Lancaster, Pa., p. 307
Gravestone Inscriptions, Hershey Cemetery, Hershey, Pa.
Gravestone Inscriptions, Spring Creek Cemetery, Hershey, Pa.
Lebanon County, Pa. Orphans Court, Marriage License Docket, Vol. 5, p. 59
Ibid., Vol. 25, p. 153
Lebanon Daily News, Lebanon, Pa., March 12, 1945, December 9, 1970
Office of the Prothonotary for the County of Lebanon, Index of Divorce,
    p. H-1

96. ELIZABETH LONGENECKER EBERSOLE [Elias A.[5], John[4], Jacob.[3], John[2], Jacob[1]], daughter of Elias A. and Catharine (Longenecker) Ebersole, was born August 3, 1872 in Londonderry Township, Lebanon County, Pa. Elizabeth died December 13, 1946 at Palmyra, Lebanon County, Pa. She is buried at the Spring Creek Cemetery, Hershey, Dauphin County, Pa.

Elizabeth (better known as Lizzie) was married to John Adam Kiefer on June 28, 1890 at Annville, Lebanon County, Pa. John Adam,(better known as Adam) was the son of Jeremiah and Anna Kiefer. He was born June 26, 1869 in Londonderry Township, Lebanon County, Pa.. Adam died October 19, 1915 and is buried at the Spring creek Cemetery, Hershey, Pa.

Issue: (all born in Lebanon County, Pa.)

122.   i. Susan E., b. 1891
123.   ii. Clarence, b. 1893
124.   iii. Charles E., b. 1894
125..   iv. Grant E., b. 1905
                v. Katharine who married Harry Bowman and had a
                   daughter Eleanor. Nothing more is known about
                   Katharine and her family.

References:

Inscriptions, Spring Creek Cemetery, Hershey, Pa.
Keefer, Russell C., Personal interview
Lebanon County, Pa., Orphans Court, Marriage License Docket, Vol. 4,
      p. 291
Lebanon Daily News, Lebanon, Pa., December 15, 1946, April 21, 1948
Lebanon Valley Register, Palmyra, Pa., December 19, 1946
Records of Christ Reformed Church, Annville, Pa.

97. SUSAN P. EBERSOLE [Elias A.[5], John[4], Jacob.[3], John[2], Jacob[1]], daughter of Elias A. and Catharine (Longenecker) Ebersole, was born June 15, 1874 near Palmyra, Lebanon County, Pa. She died November 15, 1893 in childbirth, according to family members.. She is buried in the United Brethren Cemetery, Campbelltown, Lebanon County, Pa.

On June 17, 1893, Susan was married to Abner E. Sellers. Abner was born April 2, 1868 in Dauphin County, Pa. He died February 11, 1928 and is buried at the Mt. Annville Cemetery, Annville, Pa.

Issue:

126.   i. Pearl S., b. October 14, 1893

After the death of Susan, Abner Sellers married Anna S. Kiefer. Anna was born August 5, 1872. She died January 19, 1942 and is buried at the Mt. Annville Cemetery, Annville, Pa.

Issue:

127.   i. Rhoda K., b. August 15, 1897

Note that Rhoda was a half-sister to Pearl. They had the same father but

70

different mothers.

References:

Inscriptions, Mt. Annville cemetery, Annville, Pa.
Inscriptions, United brethren Cemetery, Campbelltown, Pa.
Lebanon County, Pa., Orphans Court, Marriage License Docket, Vol. 6, p. 406
Ibid., Vol. 28, p. 44
Lebanon Daily News, Lebanon, Pa., February 13, 1928, December 26, 1957

98. ISAAC LONGENECKER EBERSOLE Elias A.[5], John[4], Jacob.[3], John[2], Jacob[1]], son of Elias A. and Catharine (Longenecker) Ebersole, was born November 27, 1883 in Londonderry Township, Lebanon County, Pa. He died October 17, 1964 at Palmyra, Lebanon County, Pa. Isaac is buried in the Hanoverdale Cemetery, Hanoverdale, Dauphin County, Pa.

Isaac was married to Minerva C. Groff, daughter of John and Amanda (Conrad) Groff. Minerva was born July 31, 1889 in East Hanover Township, Dauphin County, Pa. She died December 30, 1980 at Lebanon, Pa. and is buried with her husband at the Hanoverdale Cemetery.

Isaac Ebersole was a carpenter. He and his family were members of the Hanoverdale Church of the Brethren.

Issue:

 i. Grace A. b. 1909. Grace was married July 25, 1931 to Harold H. G. Peiffer, son of Howard J. and Elsie M. (Haas) Peiffer, at Annville, Lebanon County, Pa. Haro was born in 1911 at Union Deposit, Dauphin County, Pa.
  Grace and her husband worked at the Hershey Chocolate Factory.

 ii. Viola who married James Skinner.

 iii. Raymond J. b. October 8, 1913; d. January 19. 1914.

 iv. Harold W., b. July 8, 1923; d. February 21, 1938.

 v. Kenneth L., b. April 12, 1928; d. June 20, 1940.
  Kenneth's death was caused by a fall from a tree.
  Raymond, Harold and Kenneth are all buried at the Hanoverdale Cemetery.

References:

Ebersole family papers
Inscriptions, Hanoverdale Cemetery, Hanoverdale, Pa.

Lebanon County, Pa. Orphans Court, Marriage License Docker, Vol. 35, p. 476
Lebanon Daily News, Lebanon, Pa., March 18, 1964, December 30, 1980

99. SADIE EBERSOLE [Jacob [Jacob A.[5], John M.[4]. Jacob B.[3], John[2], Jacob[1]], daughter of Jacob A. and Mary Ann (Emerich) Ebersole, was born April 30, 1877 in Londonderry Township, Lebanon County, Pa. She died February 26, 1813 and is buried at the Gravel Hill Cemetery, Palmyra, Lebanon County, Pa.

On December 30, 1893, Sadie was married to Ulysses S. Ricker at Palmyra, Lebanon County, Pa. Ulysses, son of Henry and Elizabeth Ricker was born December 10, 1859 in Lebanon County, Pa. He died November 5, 1948 and is buried at the Gravel Hill Cemetery with his wife.

Issue:

    i. blanche M., b. July 23, 19894; d. unmarried February 24, 1966.. Bur. at Gravel Hill Cemetery.
    ii. Arthur E., b. February 1,1897; d. October 13, 1909.
    iii. Mary E., b. November 3, 1898; d. December 24, 1898
    iv. Claude J., b. August 28, 1901; d. January 31, 1953.
    v. Infant daughter, b. 1906. This child may have been a stillborn.
    vi. Ralph R., b.
    vii. J. henry, b.

References:
Daily Report, Lebanon, Pa., January 2, 1894
Ebersole, Mabel, handwritten family record
Gravestone inscriptions, Gravel Hill Cemetery, Palmyra, Pa.
Lebanon County, Pa. Orphans Court, Marriage License docket, Vol. 7 p.37

100. ELIZABETH EBERSOLE [John G.[5,] Jacob M.[4], Jacob B.[3], John[2], Jacob[1]], daughter of John G. and Sylvanus Hatton Ebersole, was born, according to family records, October 18, 1873 at Hockersville, Dauphin County, Pa. Records of the Lebanon County Board of Health indicate that she was born at Lawn, Lebanon County, Pa. She died in 1969 and is buried in the cemetery adjoining Stauffer's Mennonite church, Bachmanville, Dauphin county, Pa.

Elizabeth was married December 11, 1896 to Fred W. Kreiiner at

Lebanon, Lebanon County, Pa. Fred, the son of W. F. and Mary Kreiner, was born January 2, 1859 at Lebanon, Lebanon County, Pa. He died December 6, 1933 at Lebanon, Pa. and is buried at the Mt. Lebanon Cemetery, Lebanon, Pa.

Fred Kreiner was a practicing dentist at Lebanon.

Issue:

> i. Ezra E., b. July 25, 1898; d. 1976. bur. Stauffer's Mennonite Cemetery, Bachmanville, Pa.
>
> ii. John E., b. May 9, 1897; d. young

References:

Ebersole, John G., family bible
Inscriptions, Mt. Lebanon Cemetery, Lebanon, Pa.
Inscriptions, Stauffer's Mennonite Cemetery, Bachmanville, Pa.
Kreiner, Fred, family bible
Lebanon County, Pa., Orphans Court, Marriage License Docket, Vol.9, p. 94
Lebanon Daily News, Lebanon, Pa., October 9, 1869
Record of births Reported to the Lebanon County Board of Health, p.53, No. 2115
Record of Marriages Reported to the Lebanon Count board of Health April 10, 1892 to April 14, 1906, p.16

101. MOSES HATTON EBERSOLE [John G.[5,] Jacob M.[4], Jacob B.[3], John[2], Jacob[1]], son of John G. and Sylvanus (Hatton) Ebersole, was born January 6, 1876 at Lawn, Lebanon County, Pa. He died April 3, 1948 and is buried at Stauffer's Mennonite Cemetery, Bachmanville, Dauphin County, Pa.

Moses was married November 22, 1906 to Elisabeth Lehman Longenecker. Elisabeth, daughter of Samuel E. and susan s. (Lehman) Longenecker, was born December 19, 1882. She died June 19, 1967 at Elizabethtown, Lancaster county, Pa. and is buried with her husband at Stauffer's Mennonite Cemetery.

Issue:

> i. Lester Longenecker, b. August 14, 1907. There is a gravestone at Stauffer's Mennonite Cemetery with the dates 1907 and 1984 that is believed to have been erected to the memory of Lester. Lester was married to Martha Riegel who was born August 7, 1908.

ii. Ruth Longenecker, b. October 23, 1908. Ruth was married to Howard M. Musser January 29, 1936 at Deodate, Dauphin County, Pa. Howard was born in West Hempfield Township, Lancaster County, Pa. October 19, 1910. He died July 22, 1975. Howard was the son of Enos S. and Anna Musser.

iii. Edith Longenecker, b February 20, 1910. Edith married Jonas B. Groff November 21, 1932 at Deodate, Dauphin County, Pa. Jonas, son of Phares K. and Susie (Baker) Groff, was born May 5, 1911 in Rapho Township, Lancaster County, Pa.

iv. Susan Longenecker, b. January 28, 1912

v. Jacob Longenecker, b. August 3, 1914. Jacob married Alverta Musser who was born September 25, 19145.

vi. Abner Longenecker, b. May 18, 1917 at Elizabethtown, Lancaster County, Pa. Abner married June 30, 1945 to Emma Mae Ginder. Emma was born in Rapho Township, Lancaster County, Pa. December 10, 1917, the daughter of Phares and Annie (Hoffer) Ginder. She died September 17, 1968. She and her husband are both buried at Stauffer's Mennonite Cemetery, Bachmanville, Pa.
After Emma died, Abner married a second time to Anna Mae Stauffer.

vii. Ada Longenecker, b. May 27, 1919; d. October 9, 1981. Ada was married to Raymond S. Baum.

viii. Moses Longenecker, b. January 29, 1922. Moses married to Elma M. Hertzler, daughter of Owen A. and Alta (Burkhart) Hertzler. Elma was born November 24, 1921.

ix. John Irvin, b. April 11, 1924. John married Mildred E. Hoffer, daughter of Christ H. and Margie (Greiner) Hoffer.

References:

Die Lebanon Volks=Zeitung, Lebanon, Pa., January 28, 1906
Inscriptions, Stauffer'sMennonite Cemetery, Bachmanville, Pa.
Lancaster County, Pa. Orphans Court, Marriage License Docket, Book 6, Book F, Vol. 6,, License No. 15012
Ibid., Vol. G, License No. 16353
Lancaster County, Pa. Wills, Will of Lizzie L. Ebersole, File No. 604, 1967

Lebanon County, Pa., Orphans Court, Marriage License Docket, Vol. 17, p.95

Lebanon Daily News, Lebanon, Pa., October 12, 1881

Zeager, Lloyd, *The Shope Mennonite Cemetery and Area Families,*
    Pennsylvania Mennonite Heritage, Lancaster, Pa., Vol. 6, no.1, pp.7,
    8, 19, 21

102. SUSANNA H. EBERSOLE [John G.[5,] Jacob M.[4], Jacob B.[3], John[2], Jacob[1]], daughter of John G. and Sylvanus (Hatton) Ebersole, was born September 17, 1878, probably in Lebanon County, Pa. She died January 29, 1975 and is buried in the churchyard of Stauffer's Mennonite Church, Bachmanville, Dauphin County, Pa.

On November 17, 1899 Susanna was married Jacob G. Shenk at Lawn, Lebanon County, Pa. Jacob was born April 29, 1878. He died August 1, 1942.

Issue:

    i. Estelle who married Herman Landis.
    ii. Walter, b.
    iii. John, b.
    iv. Mary, b.

References:

Inscriptions, Stauffer's Mennonite Cemetery, Bachmanville,, Pa.

Lancaster County, Pa., Orphans Court, Marriage License Docket, 16080

103. JOHN H. EBERSOLE [John G.[5,] Jacob M.[4], Jacob B.[3], John[2], Jacob[1]], son of John G. and Sylvanus (Hatton) Ebersole, was born August 1, 1899 in Lebanon County, Pa., probably in the vicinity of Lawn. He died January 30, 1963 at Hershey, Dauphin County, Pa.

John was married September 16, 1916 to Lillian Boger at Lebanon, Lebanon County, Pa. Lillian, daughter of John B. and Rebecca (winters) Boger, was born in June of 1896. She died June 18, 1985.

John H. Ebersole was a street car conductor.

Issue:

    i. Dorothy, b. February 27, 1917
    ii. Harry, b. October 15, 1918; d. October 26, 1918
    iii. Russell, b. January 19, 1920; d. January 22,1920
    iv. Paul, b. July, 2, 1922; d. July 2, 1922
    v. Harold J., b. October 19, 1923

vi. Eleanor Ruth, b. July, 23, 1923
References:
Inscriptions, Christ Lutheran Church, Bellegrove, Lebanon County, Pa.
Lebanon Count, Pa., Orphans Court Index
Lebanon County, Pa., Orphans Court, Marriage License Docket, Vol. 25,
    p. 381
Lebanon Daily News, Lebanon, Pa., January 31,1963

104. PHOEBE H. EBERSOLE [John G.[5,] Jacob M.[4], Jacob B.[3], John[2],
Jacob[1]], daughter of John G. and Sylvanus (Hatton) Ebersole, was born April
4, 1894 at Lawn, Lebanon County, Pa. Phoebe died February 11, 1984 at
Annville, Lebanon County, Pa. She is buried at the Grave Hill Cemetery,
Palmyra, Pa.

    Phoebe was married November 22, 1913 to Ammon s. Fasnacht at Lawn,
Lebanon County, Pa. Ammon, son of David and Frances (Garman) Fasnacht,
was born December 7, 1893. He died June 2, 1978 and is buried with his
wife at the Gravel Hill Cemetery.
    Issue:
        i. Ralph E., b. September 18, 1916 at Campbelltown,
            Lebanon County, Pa. He died February 27, 1983. Ralph
            was married to Susan Behrens.
        ii. Paul E., b. April 4, 1919
        iii. Lloyd J., b. June 18, 1921
    References:
Ebersole, John G., family bible
Inscriptions, Gravel Hill Cemetery, Palmyra, Pa.
Lebanon County, Pa.,Orphans Court, Marriage License Docket, Vol. 23, p.
129
The Daily News, Lebanon, Pa., February 28, 1983, February 13, 1984

105. MARY G. EBERSOLE [Samuel M.[5], Jacob M.[4], Jacob B.[3],
John[2], Jacob[1]], daughter of Samuel Moyer and Isabella (Gruber) Ebersole,
was born April 27, 1896 at Lawn, Lebanon County, Pa. The date of Mary's
death and place of burial are not now known.
    Mary married January 20, 1913 to Paris L. Koser. Paris, son of Abner A.
Koser, was born in 1894 in Rapho Township, Lancaster County, Pa. He died
in 1953 and is buried in the Crossroads Cemetery at Mt. Joy, Lancaster
County, Pa.

Issue:

i. Vivian e., b. June 4, 1927 in Lancaster County, Pa. She died March 25, 1933 and is buried in the Crossroads Cemetery.

References:
Inscriptions, Crossroads Cemetery, Mt. Joy, Pa.
Lancaster County, Pa. Orphans Court, Marriage License Docket, Book U, Vol. 3, p. 5931

106. LLOYD B. EBERSOLE [David M.[5], Jacob M.[4], Jacob B.[3], John[2], Jacob[1]], son of David M. and Alice S. (Brandt) Ebersole, was born at Middletown, Dauphin county, Pa. in 1902. The date of his death and place of burial are not now known.

On March 28, 1924, Lloyd was married to Margaret Halbleib at Mt. Joy, Lancaster County, Pa. Margaret, daughter of Henry J. and Cora A. (Clouser) Halbleib, was born in 1906.

Issue: (all born in Lancaster County, Pa.)

i. Norman Clayman, b. 1926 in Mt. Joy Township
ii. Jay Raymond, b. 1929 in Mt. Joy Township
iii. Harry J. b. 1937 at Elizabethtown
iv. Lloyd B. Jr.,b. October 21, 1939
v. Anna Mary, b. December 12, 1941
vi. Dorothy Kline, b. January 26, 19455 at Mt. Joy

References:
Lancaster County, Pa. Marriage License Docket, Book d, Vol. 5, License No. 1901

107. AMOS R. EBERSOLE. [Levi L.[5], John D.[4], David[3], Jacob[2], Jaocb[1]], son of Levi L. and Mary N. (Risser) Ebersole, was born December 22, 1870 in West Donegal Township, Lancaster County, Pa. He died February 7, 1964 and is buried at Good's Mennonite Cemetery, near Elizabethtown, Lancaster County, Pa.

Amos was married to Clara Whisler on December 5, 1891 at Mt. Joy, Lancaster County, Pa. Clara, daughter of Benjamin Whisler, was born June 8, 1871 in Cumberland County, Pennsylvania. She died April 3, 1925 and is buried with her husband in Good's Mennonite Cemetery.

After the death of Clara, Amos married a second time to Martha E. Fry, widow of John W. Fry. Martha, daughter of Christian and Mary Ebersol, was born January 31, 1880 in Conoy Township, Lancaster County, Pa. Martha died January 23, 1945 and is buried in Good's Mennonite Cemetery with her husband. There os no known issue from his second marriage.

Amos R. Ebersole and his family were farmers.

Issue:

    i. Dora W., b. January 20, 1889; d. May 20, 1893

    ii. Amos W., b. April 4, 1894 at Srasburg, Lancaster County, Pa. He died March 26, 1952. These are the dates on the gravestone. The Lancaster County Record of births gives date of birth as September 20, 1894..

    iii. Jonas W., b. August 29, 1895 in West Donegal Township, Lancaster County, Pa. in West Donegal Township, Lancaster County, Pa. He died February 16, 1979 and is buried at Good's Mennonite Cemetery. Jonas had married Lillian H. Risser on October 11, 1917 Township, Lancaster county, Pa. Lillian was born in 1896 in Londonderry Township, Lebanon County, Pa.

    iv. Nora W., b. 1897 in West Donegal Township

    v. Levi W., b. December 9, 1899 at Elizabethtown, Lancaster County, Pa.

    vi. Walter Whisler, b. August 15, 1901 in Conoy Township

    vii. Mary W., b. 1904 in West Donegal Township

    viii. Clarence, b. July 29, 1907

References:

Gerberich, Albeit H., *Gravestone Inscriptions, Good's Meeting House Cemetery*

Inscriptions, Good's Mennonite Cemetery, near Elizabthtown, Pa.

Lancaster County, Pa. Orphans Court, Marriage License Docket, Book L, License No. 6848

Ibid., Book K. Vol. 4, License No. 5766

  :   Book N, vol. 5, License No. 6896

Lancaster County, Pa., Record of Births

    108. FANNIE R. EBERSOLE [Levi L.[5], John D.[4], David[3], Jacob[2], Jaocb[1]], daughter of Levi L. and Mary N. (Risser) Ebersole, was born about 1878 in West Donegal Township, Lancaster County, Pa.

On November 12, 1894, Fannie was married to Joseph H. Nissley. Joseph

was born about 1870 in Londonderry Township, Dauphin County, Pa.
Issue:

i. Paul E., b. January 2, 1915; d. December 26, 1965..
Paul was married November 16, 1937 to Esther B.
Miller.
References:
Huss, Arlene et al, *The David and Anna Miller Story*, p..284
Lancaster County, Pa., Orphans Court, Marriage License Docket, Book R,
License No. 10254

109. MARTIN R. EBERSOLE [Levi L.[5] , John D.[4], David[3], Jacob[2],
Jaocb[1]], son of Levi L. and Mary N.(Risser) Ebersole, was born February 8,
1879 in West Donegal Township, Lancaster County, Pa. He died March 25,
1954 and is buried at Good's Mennonite Cemetery, near Elizabethtown,
Lancaster County, Pa.
    Martin was married November 18, 1897 to Lissie H. Risser. Lissie was
born in 1876 and died in 1952.
Issue: (all born in Lancaster County, Pa.)

i. Abraham Risser, b. November 25, 1898. On October 5,
1926 Abraham was married to Frances E. Shank.
ii. Elam Risser, b. November 22, 1902. Elam married
Mabel Saylor.
iii. Jacob Risser, b. June 5, 1907
iv. Ira Risser, b. May 15, 1917. Ira married Beulah
Bollenger
References:
Coble, Anna Mae Meckley, *Family of Martin Nissley Risser(1850-1926) and
his wife Maria Brubaker Horst*, pp. 24, 25
Heisey, Luther M., *The Heisey Family in America*, p. 19
History of the Longacre-Longaker-Longenecker Family, pp. 13-133
Inscriptions, Good's Mennonite Cemetery, near Elizabethtown
Lancaster County, Pa.,Orphans Court, Marriage License Docket, Book,
Vol. 5, License No. 5423
Ibid., Book Y, License No. 13720
Lancaster County, Pa., Record of Births
Lancaster, Pa., Wills, Will File No. 495, 1954

110. SETH E. EBERSOLE [Peter C.[5], Christian K.[4], Jacob M.[3], [Jacob],

Jacob], son of Peter C. and Mary (Eby) Ebersole, was born January 1, 1868 in Lancaster County, Pa. he died October 3, 1935 at Lancaster, Lancaster County, Pa. and is buried at the Landisville Mennonite Cemetery, Landisville, Lancaster County, Pa.

On October 24, 1889, Seth was married to Martha Rutt Stauffer at Manheim, Lancaster County, Pa.

Seth Ebersole was ordained a Mennonite preacher on August 15, 1918

Issue:

  i. Henry S., b. November 25, 1918 at Lancaster, Pa.
  ii. Barbara Stauffer, b. 1893 in Rapho Township, La caster County, Pa.
  iii. Benjamin S., b. 18894 in West Hempfield Township, Lancaster County, Pa.
  iv. A son born November 18, 1897 in West Hempfield township; d. November 18, 1897 and is buried in the Landisville Mennonite Cemetery.
  v. Christian S., b. September 18, 1900 at Landisville
  vi. Norman S., b. March 11, 1903 in Rapho Township, Lancaster County, Pa.
  vii. Mary Stauffer, b. 1906 in East Hempfield Township, Lancaster County, Pa.
  viii. Bertha s., b. 1908 in East Hempfield Township

References:
Inscriptions, Landisville Cemetery, Landisville, Pa.
Lancaster County, Pa. Orphans Court, Marriage License Docket, Book H, Vol. 1, 4325

111, CORA GINGRICH EBERSOLE [Jacob E.[5], Daniel[4], Jacob[3], Martin[2], Jacob[1]], daughter of Jacob E. and Kate (Gingrich) Ebersole, was born September 28, 1883 in North Annville Township, Lebanon County, Pa. She died October 27, 1971 and is buried at Gingrich's Mennonite Cemetery, North Cornwall township, Lebanon County, Pa...

Cora was married to Samuel J. Tennis on November 12, 1910 at the residence of Mennonite Bishop Noah Annville, Lebanon County, Pa. Samuel, the son of Samuel J. and Fannie (Fackler) Tennis,, was born March 10, 1879 at Hanoverdale, Dauphin County, Pa.. He died April 13, 1966 and is buried at Gingrich's Mennonite Cemetery, with his wife.

Issue;

          i. Katie Dorcas, b. December 26, 1911; d. January 17,
             1912.
             Bur. Gingrich's Mennonite Cemetery, North Cornwall
             Township, Lebanon Country, Pa.
128.   ii. Jacob Samuel, b. May 1, 1913.
         iii. Christian Ebersole. September 15, 1915; d. July 14,
              1916. Buried Gingrich's Mennonite Cemetery
         iv. Joseph Irvin, b. April 29, 1919; d. 1921; d. November
             21, 1921. Bur. at Gingrich's Mennonite Cemetery.
129.   v. Mary Elizabeth, b. August 28, 1923;
    References:
Gordon, John D., *The Family of Jacob and Kate Ebersole*
Lebanon County, Pa., Orphans Court, Marriage License Docket, Vol. 20, p.
     188
Ibid.,, Vol. 48, p. 435
Walters, Mollie, Correspondence

    112. IRVIN GINGRICH EBERSOLE [Jacob E.[5], Daniel[4], Jacob[3],
Martin[2], Jacob[1]], son of Jacob E. and Kate (Gingrich) was born June 29,
1885 in North Annville Township, Lebanon County, Pa. He died April 17,
1933 at Cleona, Lebanon County, Pa. and is buried in the cemetery of the
Midway Church of the Brethren in South .Lebanon Township, Lebanon
County, Pa.
    Irvin married Vara May Hunsucjer, daughter of Frank and Lizzie L.
(Zimmerman) Hunsicker January 18, 1913.. Vara was born March 20, 1891
in Bethel Township, Lebanon County, Pa. Vara died September, 1966 and is
buried with her husband at the Midway Church of the Brethren.
     Issue:
130.   i. Mervin Richard, b. July 21, 1920
131   ii. Irene Mae, b. August 16, 1924
    References;
Gordon, John d., *The Family of Jacob and Kate Ebersole*
Inscriptions, Cemetery adjoining the Midway Church of the Brethren in South
     Lebanon Township, Lebanon County, Pa.
Lebanon County, Pa. Orphans Court ,Marriage License Docket, Vol. 22,
     p. 147

    113. AMMON GINGRICH EBERSOLE [Jacob E.[5], Daniel[4], Jacob[3],

Martin², Jacob¹], son of Jacob E. and Kate (Gingrich) Ebersole, was born April 7, 1887 in North Annville Township, Lebanon County, Pa. He died September 23, 1968 and is buried at Gingrich's Mennonite Cemetery, North Cornwall Township, Lebanon County< Pa.

Ammon married Amanda Gingrich Horst October 24, 1908 in North Annville Township, Lebanon County, Pa. Amanda, daughter of Peter and Amanda (Gingrich) Horst, was born February 1, 1888 in South Annville Township, Lebanon County, Pa. She died April 2, 1961 and is buried at Gingrich' Mennonite Cemetery, in North Cornwall Township, Lebanon County, Pa.

Ammon and Amanda were separated in 1945.

Issue: (all born in Lebanon County, Pa.)

132.	i.	Elmer Henry, b. August 12, 1909 in South Annville Township
133.	ii.	Kathryn Esther, b. April 21, 1911 in North Annville Township
134.	iii.	Ruth Elizabeth, b. August 22, 1912 in North Cornwall Township
135.	iv.	Ammon Jacob, b. March 22,1914
	v.	Mary Amanda, b. October 2, 1915; d. January 17, 1916. Bur. Gingrich's Mennonite Cemetery, North Cornwall Township
136.	vi.	Martha May, b. September 10, 1916 in North Annville Township
	vii.	Irvin Peter, b. December 2, 1917 in North Annville Township; d. December 9, 1917. Bur. Gingrich's Mennonite Cemetery.
	viii.	Mark Horst, b. December 31, 1919 in North Annville Township; d. January 13, 1920. Bur. Gingrich's Mennonite Cemetery
137.	ix.	Aaron Harold, b. April 1, 1921 in North Annville Township
138.	x..	Paul Herman, b. November 29, 1918 in North Annville Township
	xi..	Cora Amy, b. , b. May 22, 1922 in North Annville Township, Lebanon County, Pa. On June 6, 1964, Cora was married to Carl R. Gerber at Fairmount,

Belmont County, Ohio. Carl, the son of Peter P. and Anna J. (Hostetter) Gerber, was born March 5, 1907 in Wayne County, Ohio. He died September 24, 1987 at Kidron, Ohio. The Gerbers were Mennonites.

xii. Leroy Harvey, b. July 11, 1923 in North Annville Township, Lebanon Coney, Pa. He died October 2, 1923 and is buried at Gingrich's Mennonite Cemetery.

139..   xii. Norman Joseph, b. July 13, 1928 in North Annville Township

References:
Gordon, John D., *The Jacob and Kate Ebersole Family*
Lebanon Courier, Lebanon, Pa., October 30, 1897
Lebanon Daily News, Lebanon, Pa., September 23, 1968

114. ELIZABETH EBERSOLE [Jacob E.[5], Daniel[4], Jacob[3], Martin[2], Jacob[1]], daughter of Jacob E. and Kate(Gingrich) Ebersole, was born February 22,1889 in North Annville Township, Lebanon County, Pa. She died February 14,1961 and is buried at Gingrich's Mennonite Cemetery in North Cornwall Township, Lebanon County, Pa.

On January 23, 1915, Elizabeth was married to Calvin Harrison Shuey. Calvin, son of Edward and Rosanna (Boyer) Shuey, was born July 13, 1888 at Lickdale, Lebanon County, Pa. Calvin died June 8, 1967 and is buried with his wife at Gingrich's Mennonite Cemetery.
Elizabeth and her husband were farmers.

Issue:

i. Jacob Edward, b. April 22, 1916.
ii. David Calvin, b. November 22, 1917.
iii. Viola May, b. November 18, 1919.
iv. Anna Elizabeth, b. May 29, 1922

References:
Gordon, John D., *The Jacob and Kate Ebersole Family*
Lebanon County, Pa. Orphans CXourt, Marroage :icense Docket, Vol. 24,
     p. 155

115. CLAYTON G. EBERSOLE [Jacob E.[5], Daniel[4], Jacob[3], Martin[2], Jacob[1]], son of Jacob E. and Kate Gingrich) Ebersole, was born September 26, 1890 at Annville, Lebanon County, Pa. Clayton died December 29, 1946

and is buried at the United Zion Cemetery in North Annville Township, Lebanon
County, Pa.

On January 6, 1913, Clayton was married to Ella M. Wolf at Annville, Lebanon County, Pa. Ella, the daughter of Daniel and Rosanna (Rutter) Wolf, was born about 1892 in Lebanon County, Pa. Ella died March 23, 1980 and is buried with her husband in the United Zion Cemetery.

Issue: (all born in Lebanon County, Pa.)

 i. Emma Verna, b. October 10, 1914 in South Annville Township
 ii. Roy Irvin, b. November 21, 1916 in North Annville Township
 iii. Martin William, b. July 21, 1919 in South Annville Township
 iv. Anna Myrl, b. March 28, 1925 at Annville

References:

Gordon, John d., *The Jacob and Kate Ebersole Family*

Lebanon County, Pa. Orphans Court, Marriage License Docket, Vol. 23, p. 224

116. EDNA MAE EBERSOLE [Jacob E.[5], Daniel[4], Jacob[3], Martin[2], Jacob[1]], daughter of Jacob E. and Kate (Gingrich) Ebersole, was born January 19, 1894 in North Annville Township, Lebanon County, Pa. She died September 9, 1979 at Lebanon, Lebanon County, P. She is buried at the Grand View Memorial Park, Annville, Lebanon County,,Pa..

Edna married John McKinley Gordon on April 19, 1919 at Hershey, Dauphin County, Pa. John was born March 7, 1897 in Dauphin County, Pa.,, the son of John David and Anna Rebecca (Cooper) Gordon. He died August 19, 1965 at Hershey. He is buried with his wife at the Grand view Memorial Park, Annville, Pa..

Issue:

140.   i. John David, b. December 7, 1925

References:

Gordon, John D., correspondence

117. FRANY IRENE EBERSOLE [Clinton[6], Elias A.[5], John[4], Jacob.[3], John[2], Jacob[1]], daughter of Clinton L. and Fannie K. (Shanaman) Ebersole, was born January 1, 1893 at Annville, Lebanon County, Pa. She died at

Annville, Pa., June 19, 1984 and is buried at the Grand View Memorial Park, Annville, Pa.

Frany was a name she didn't like and she rarely used. it.

On December 27, 1919, Irene was married to Arthur Stine Heilman., son of Grant and Mariah (Stine) Heilman. Arthur was born January 8, 1892. He died October 30, 1984 at Annville, Pa. He os buried with his wife at the Grand View Memorial Park.

During World War I Artur served in the U. S. Army both here and in France. He was honorably discharged with the rank of corporal.

Irene and her husband both worked in the handkerchief industry., she as a sewing machine operator and he as foreman of the finishing department at the H. O. Stansbury Co., Lebanon,Pa.

Issue: (all born in LebanonCounty, Pa.)

141.	i.	Robert Arthur, b. October 13, 1920
	ii.	Nancy Janice, b. 5, 1924 (stillborn)
142.	iii.	Nancy Janice, b. October 23, 1928

References:

Ebersole, Clinton L., family bible
Heilman, F. Irene, Personal interview
Heilman, Robert A.,Personal knowledge
Lebanon County, Pa., Orphans Court, Marriage Licens Docket, Vol. 28,
    p. 481

118. ELLA M. EBERSOLE. [Allen L.6, Elias A.5, John4, Jacob.3, John2, Jacob1], daughter of Allen L. and Minerva E. (Mutch)Ebersole, was born September 16, 1893 in South Annville township, Lebanon County, Pa. She died October 28, 1980 at Neffsville, Lancaster County, Pa. Ella is buried at the Spring Creek Cemetery, Hershey, Dauphin County, Pa.

Ella M. Ebersole was married to the Rev. Frank Stauffer Carper, D. D. on December 22, 1916. Frank, the son of Allen B. and Fannie (Stauffer) Carper on August 12, 1893 at Lebanon, Lebanon County, Pa. He died May 26, 1975 and is buried at the Spring Creek Cemetery, Hershey, Pa.

Ella was a seamstress in her early years. After her marriage to the Rev. Carper, she was active in the affairs of the Community and the Palmyra Church of the Brethren, her husbands church. Her husband was an ordained minister in the Church of the Brethren.

Issue: (all born in Lebanon County, Pa.)

143.	i.	Ruth E., b. December 5,1917

ii. Anna M., b. August 13, 1919 at Palmyra, Pa. She died unmarried October 8, 2004 at Neffsville, Lancaster County, Pa. and is buried at the Spring Creek Cemetery,.
Hershey, Pa. anna was a graduate of Elizabethtown College and the University of Columbia. She was employed by Elizabethtown Collage, Elizabethtown, Pa. as director of the college library.

144. iii. Miriam Naomi, b. 1923

145.. iv. John M., b. 2026

References:

Carper, F. S.,*History ofthe Palmyra Church of the Brethren 18892-1967*
  Printed by Forry and Hacker, Lancaster, Pa.
Inscriptions, Spring Creek Cemetery, Hershey, Pa.
Lebanon County, Pa. Orphans Court, Marriage License Docket, Vol. 4, p. 489
Ibid., Vol. 46, p.19
Lebanon Daily News, Lebanon, Pa., October 29, 1980, October 11, 2004
The Brethren Encyclopedia, Vol. III, p. 1581

119. HARRY M. EBERSOLE [Allen L.6, Elias A.[5], John[4], Jacob.[3], John[2], Jacob[1]], son of Allen L. and Minerva (Mutch) Ebersole, was born on August 10, 1902 at Palmyra, Lebanon County, Pa. He died February 14, 1996 at Palmyra, Pa. and is buried at the Spring Creek Cemetery, Hershey, Dauphin County, Pa.

 Harry was married twice. His first wife was Bernice Myers who was born May 5, 1905. She died October 19, 1942 and is buried at the Spring Creek Cemetery.

  Issue:

146. i. Gerald R.,b. July 13, 1934

 After the death of Bernice, Harry was married on June 24, 1950 to Effie V. Wampler at Palmyra, Pa. by the Rev. Frank S. Carper. Effie, born December 2, 1912 in Rockledge County, Virginia, was the daughter of Homer J. and Delphie (Hale) Wampler.. She died September 2, 1990 and is buried at the Spring Creek Cemetery, Hershey, Pa.

 When Harry married Effie He acquired a step-son, Richard C. wampler.

 Harry M. Ebersole was the chief auto and truck mechanic for the Hershey Estates, Hershey, Pa.

References:

Carper, F. S., *History of the Palmyra Church of the Brethren 1892-1967*,
    pp. 283, 293, Printed by Hacker and Forry, Lancaster, Pa..
Inscriptions, Spring Creek Cemetery, Hershey, Pa.
Lebanon County, Pa. Orphans Court, Marriage License Docket, Vol. 52, p. 85
Ibid., vol. 57, p. 680
Lebanon Daily News, Lebanon, Pa., February 15, 1996

120. PAUL J. FORRY [Emma[6], Elias A.[5], John[4], Jacob.[3] , John[2], Jacob[1]], son of Clayton and Emma (Ebersole) Forry, was born April 28, 1892, probably in Lebanon County, Pa. He died March 20, 1963 and is buried at the Hershey Cemetery, Hershey, Dauphin County, Pa.

Paul was married to Anna M. Garman April 22, 1916 at Lebanon, Lebanon County, Pa. Anna was born November 15,1892 in Lebanon County, Pa. She died April 18, 1971 at Kansas City, Missouri and is buried with her husband at the Hershey Cemetery.

Paul Forry was a carpenter. His wife, Anna, was a stenographer. Later in life they operated a motel east of Hershey, Pa.

Issue:

    i. Mary Jane who married a man whose surname was
       Fulton and had three children. She and her family lived
       at Kansas City, Missouri.

References:

Heilman, Robert A.,Personal knowledge
Gravestone inscriptions, Hershey Cemetery, Hershey, Pa.
Lebanon County, Pa. Orphans Court, Marriage License Docket, Vol. 25,
    p. 153
Lebanon Daily News, Lebanon, Pa., March 21, 1963, April 19, 1971

121. MAGDALENA A. FORRY [Emma[6], Elias A.[5], John[4], Jacob[3], John[2], Jacob[1]], ,daughter of Clayton and Emma (Ebersole) Forry, was born, October 27, 1893 at Hershey, Dauphin County, Pa. She died December 8. 1970 at Lebanon, LebanonCounty, Pa. and is buried at the Hanoverdale Cemetery, Hanoveerdale, Dauphin County, Pa.

Magdalena, better known as Lena, was married to Christian C. Groff. Christ, the name by which he was better known, was born May 14, 1880. He died June 27, 1946 and is buried with his wife in the Hanoverdale Cemetery.

"Lena" and her family lived at Hershey, Dauphin County, Pa.
    Issue:

                    i. LeRoy L., b. 1915 at Union Deposit, Dauphin County,
                       Pa. On April 30, 1936, LeRoy married Frances V.
                       Brubaker at Palmyra, Lebanon County, Pa. Frances, the
                       daughter of Jacob and Leah (Gingrich) Brubaker was
                       born about the year 1912 at Hershey, Pa.
                   ii. Hilda J., b. about 1916, probably at Union Deposit,
                       Dauphin County, Pa. Hilda was married to Harold
                       Bowman on July 13, 1941 at Palmyra, Lebanon County,
                       Pa. Harold was born about 1911 in Lebanon County,
                       Pa.,
                       the son of John H. and Ellen E. (Heilman) Bowman.
                  iii. Naomi who married Earl L. Kuntz.

    References:

Batdorf, Virginia Faust, *The Batdorf Family*. 1990, pp. 84, 85
Carper, F. S., *History of the Palmyra church of the Brethren 18892-1967*, p
307
    Printed by Forry and Hacker, Lancaster, Pa.
Inscriptions, Hanoverdale Cemetery, Hanoverdale, Pa.
Lebanon County, Pa. Orphans Court, Marriage License Docket, Vol. 36, p.
800
Ibid., Vol. 43, p.298
Lebanon Daily News, Lebanon, Pa., October 9, 1970, October 12,1970.

    122. SUSAN EBERSOLE KIEFER [Elizabeth[6], Elias A.[5], John[4],
Jacob.[3] , John[2], Jacob[1]], daughter of John Adam and Elizabeth (Ebersole)
Kiefer, was born in 1891 in Lebanon County, Pa. She died February 23,
1958 and is buried at the Grand View Memorial Park, Annville,
LebanonCounty, Pa.

    susan was married to George E. Bell at Union Deposit, Dauphin County,
Pa on January 13, 1912. George, the son of George and Anna Bell, was born
in dauphin County, Pa. in 1891. He died January 9, 1967 and is buried with
his wife at the Grand view Memorial Park, Annville.

    George Bell was a butcher working out of a shop in Palmyra, Pa. where he
and his family resided.

    It appears that the Kiefers, parents and children changed the spelling of
their surname from Kiefer to Keefer.

Issue:

    i. Pauline who married a man whose surname was Kautz and had a daughter. Pauline and her family may have lived in Hummelstown, Dauphin County, Pa.

    ii. Ralph E. who lived in Baltimore at the time of his mother's death.

    iii.. Carl Ellis. about 1916 at Palmyra, Lebanon County, Pa. On January 19, 1943, Carl was married to Ruth Irene Shearer, daughter of Christian L. and Laura (Laber)at Palmyra, Pa. shearer at Palmyra, Pa. Ruth was born at Hummelstown, Dauphin County, in 1919. Ruth had been married previously on February 14, 19- -.This marriage ended January 19,1915 with the death of her husband.

    iv. Jay K., b.

References:

Carper, F. S., *History of the Palmyra Church of the Brethren 1892-1967*, p. 308. Printed by Forry and Hacker, Lancaster, Pa.

Lebanon County, Pa. Orphans Court, Marriage License Docket, vol. 21, p.246

Ibid., Vol. 45, p. 203

Lebanon Daily News, ,Lebanon, Pa., February 24, 25, 1958

    123. CLARENCE E. KEEFER [Elizabeth[6], Elias A.[5], John[4], Jacob.[3], John[2], Jacob[1]], son of John Adam and Elizabeth (Ebersole) Keefer, was born in 1893 at Campbelltown, Lebanon County, Pa. He died May 21, 1973 at Hanover, York County, Pa. and is buried at New Oxford, Adams County, Pa.

    Clarence married twice. His first wife was L. Bertha Weilert who died in 1952. His second wife was Eleanor Manifold Beck.

    Clarence Keefer received degrees in education from Millersville University and Columbia University. He also studied at Elizabethtown College, Gettysburg college and Penn State University.

    Clarence taught school in Lebanon County, Adams County and York County and served as principal of the New Oxford Schools and became the superintendent of the Adams County Schools, a position he held until his retirement in 1962.During World War II he served in the military. There is no known issue from either of his marriages.

References:
Keefer, Russell C., Personal knowledge
Lebanon Daily News, Lebanon, Pa., May 22, 1973

124. CHARLES EBERSOLE KEEFER [Elizabeth[6], Elias A.[5], John[4], Jacob.[3], John[2], Jacob[1]], son of John Adam and Elizabeth (Ebersole) Keefer, was born July 15, 1894 in Lebanon County, Pa. He died February 1, 1970 and is buried in the Hershey Cemetery, Hershey, Dauphin County, Pa.

Charles was married to Mabel J. Herr on June 28, 1919 at Reading, Berks County, Pa. Mabel, the daughter of David and Fannie (Brandt)Herr, was born
April 9, 1893 in Lebanon County, Pa. she died September 10, 1960 at Reading, Berks County, Pa.

Charles was associated with the Lebanon Hardware Co. at Lebanon, Pa. for 50 years. He was head of the firm at the time of his retirement in 1970.

Charles Ebersole was a veteran of World War I. He and his family lived at Lebanon, Pa.

    Issue:

147.   i. Russell C., b. January 19, 1920 at Lebanon, Pa.

    References:
Heilman, Robert A., Personal knowledge
Keefer, Russell C., Personal interview
Lebanon County, Pa Orphans Court, Marriage License Docket, Vol. 28, p. 151
Lebanon Daily News, Lebanon, Pa., February 1, 19, 1970, February 4, 1970

125. GRANT E. KEEFER [Elizabeth[6], Elias A.[5], John[4], Jacob.[3], John[2], Jacob[1]], son of John Adam and Elizabeth (Ebersole) Keefer, was born April 22,1905 in Lebanon County, Pa. He died April 22, 1978 at his residence, near Jonestown, Lebanon County, Pa. Grant is buried at the Spring Creek Cemetery, Hershey, Dauphin County, Pa.

Grant married Lizzie M. Eisenhuer, daughter of Calvin and Nena (Wenrich) Eisenhauer on August 26, 1922. Lizzie was born March 21, 1905 in LebanonCounty, Pa. she died November 9, 1987 and is buried at the Spring Creek Cemetery with her husband.

Grant was a farmer near Jonestown, Lebanon County, Pa. His wife, Lizzie, was a school teacher at the time of their marriage.

    Issue:

148,   i. Roy A., b. February 11, 1923
        References:
Gravestone inscriptions, Spring creek Cemetery, Hershey, Pa.
Keefer, Russell C., personal interview
Lebanon County, Pa. Orphans Court, Marriage License Docket, Vol. 30,
        p. 482
Lebanon Daily News, Lebanon, Pa., April 27, 1978, April 28,1978,
November
        10, 1987

        126. PEARL S. SELLERS [Susan P.[5], Elias A.[5], John[4], Jacob.[3] , John[2],
Jacob[1]],   daughter of Abner P. and Susan P. (Ebersole) Sellers was born
October 14, 1893. She died December 24, 1957 and is buried at the Mt.
Annville Cemetery, Annville, Lebanon County, Pa.
        Pearl was married to Joseph Horn October 13, 1915 at Annville, Pa.
Joseph, the son of Philip and Elizabeth (Steely) Horn, was born February 8,
1892 at Hegins,Schuylkill County, Pa. He died October 17, 1918 and is also
buried in the Mt. Annville Cemetery, Annville, Pa.
        Pearl was a bookkeeper. Her husband was a furnace installer.
        Issue:
                        i. A daughter (stillborn)
After the death of her husband, joseph, Pearl married James Jared Horn, a
brother of Joseph. The marriage took place August 30, 1923. James Jared,
son of Philip and Elizabeth (Steely) Horn, was born October 12, 1897 at
Hegins, Pa. He died November 18, 1975 and is buried with his wife at the
Mt. Annville Cemetery.
        James is a name he seldom used. He preferred to be known as Jared.
        Jared was a printer by trade. He and his family lived at Annville, Pa.
                Issue: (both born at Annville, Pa.(
149.   i. James Jared Jr., b. November 13, 1926
150.   ii. David, b. December 14, 1929
        References:
Gravestone inscriptions, Mt. Annville Cemetery, Annville, Pa.
Horn, David, Personal interview
Lebanon County, Pa. Orphans Court, Marriage License Docket, Vol. 23,
        p. 467
Ibid., Vol. 31, p.260

127. RHODA K. SELLERS [Susan P.5, Elias A.[5], John[4], Jacob.[3], John[2], Jacob[1]], daughter of Abner P. and Anna (Kiefer) Sellers, was born August 15, 1897 in Lebanon County, Pa. She died September 20, 1949 at Steeltom, Dauphin County, Pa.

On April 30, Rhoda was married at Annville, Lebanon County, Pa. to Paul V. Stober a World War I veteran and the son of Joseph P. and Catharine (Miller) Stober. Paul was born January 2, 1898, He died July 19, 1971 at Steelton, Pa. Both Rhoda and her husband are buried at the Mt. Annville Cemetery, Annville, Pa.

After Rhoda's death, Paul married Catharine Moos. Nothing more is known about Catharine.

Paul was a shoemaker. He also worked for the Bethlehem Steel Corp. at Steelton, Pa.

Issue:

        i. Grace who married Frank Sucec
      ii Marlin, b.
      iii. Earl, b..

Paul also had three step-sons, Daniel, Stanley and Samuel.

References:

Horn, David, Personal interview

Lebanon County, Pa. Orphans Court, Marriage License Docket,
    Vol. 28, p. 44

Lebanon Daily News, Lebanon, Pa., November 21, 1949, July 20, 1974

128. JACOB SAMUEL TENNIS [Cora G.[6] Jacob E.[5], Daniel[4], Jacob[3], Martin[2], Jacob[1]], sam of Samuel J. and Cora (Gingrich) Tennis, was born May 1, 1913. He died January 27, 1992 and is buried at Gingrich's Mennonite Cemetery, North Cornwall Township, Lebanon Count, Pa.

Jacob was married to Mabel E. Hertzler. at Camp Hill, Cumberland County, Pa. was born July 5, 1917 at Camp Hill, the daughter of Daniel Zimmerman and Ella (Miller) Hertzler. Jacob died January 27, 1992 and is buried at Gingrich's Mennonite Cemetery in North Cornwall Township, Lebanon County, Pa.

Jacob was a farmer and a miller.

Issue:

      i. Mervin J., b. 1942; died 1944. Bur. Gingrich's
         Mennonite Cemetery, North Cornwall Township,
         Lebanon County, Pa.

ii. Elvin L., b. 1945; d. 1945. Bur. Gingrich's Mennonite Cemetery.

iii. Miriam Esther, b. February 11, 1946. Miriam was married December 27, 1968 to Donald Mock at Wormleysburg, Cumberland County, Pa.. He was born April 21, 1940.

iv. Larry G., b. May 19, 1948. Larry was married twice. His first wife was Brenda Berglron whom he married august 7, 1970. He divorced Brenda in 1982.His second wife, Lyn Hayworth, he married July 20, 1985.

v. Elva Mae, b. June 19, 1952 at Mechanicsburg, Cumberland County, Pa. Elva married Steven Craig Biggs at Mechanicsburg on September 23, 1972..

vi. Nelson Ray, b. November 27, 1953 at Mechanicsburg, Cumberland County, Pa. Nelson was married November 24, 1978 to Leigh Rathfon at Bowmansdale, Cumberland County, Pa. Leigh, daughter of Robert Lee and Esther Pearl(Ferguson) Rathfon, was born March 11, 1961 at Harrisburg, Dauphin County, Pa.

vii. Anna Marie, b. January 22, 1956. Anna Marie was married to Roger Ritchi from whom she divorced in 1987..

viii. Donald Lee, b. November 14, 1957 at Mechanicsburg, Cumberland County, Pa. On April 25, 1981, he was married to Connie Ann Sholly at Bowmansdale, Pa. Connie was born January 19, 1962, the daughter of Harold and Sandra Sholly.

ix. Carol Ann, b. November 29, 1959. Carol was married February 11, 1955 to Jim Mull.

References:
Gordon, John D., *The Family of Jacob and Kate Ebersole*

129. MARY ELIZABETH TENNIS [Cora G.[6] Jacob E.[5], Daniel[4], Jacob[3], Martin[2], Jacob[1]], daughter of Samuel J. and Cora G. (Ebersole) Tennis, was born August 28, 1923;

Mary was married to John A. Moonshine December 14, 1945 in North Annville Township, Lebanon County, Pa. John A., the son of George D. and Sallie (Schaeffer) Moonshine, was born June 8, 1912 at Annville, Lebanon

County, Pa. He died November 17, 1978 and is buried at Grand View Memorial Park, Annville, Pa. John A. and Mary Elizabeth were divorced in 1960 and Mary Elizabeth subsequently married Clair A. Beam on July 25, 1963 at Palmyra, Pa. Clair, the son of Phoebe Beam was born December 2, 1914. They were divorced in 1987.

Issue:

i. John Leroy, b. March 6, 1947 at Lebanon, Lebanon County, Pa. He Married Sherry Gail Goodwin September . Sherry was born May 7, 1954 at Elkton, Maryland, the daughter of Basil and Loretta (Ailshire) Goodwin..

ii. Sherman Daniel, b. March 14, 1948. On April 12, 1970 he married Brenda Jean

iii. Sherrie Lynn, b. September 22, 1960 at Lebanon, Pa. Sherrie married Edward Grelberis.

The following children were born from Mary Elizabeth's second marriage.

iv. Ronald Clair, b. August 23, 1946

v. Linda Jean, b. July 29, 1948. John Gordon notes that Linda is a step-child.

vi. Christine Ann, b. November 12, 1950. (step-child)

vii. Albert Floyd, b. November 25, 1967

References:

Gordon, John D., *The Family of Jacob and Kate Ebersole*

Lebanon County, Pa. Orphans Court, Marriage License Docket, Vol. 48, p. 435

130. MERVIN RICHARD EBERSOLE [Irvin G.[7,] Cora G.[6] Jacob E.[5], Daniel[4], Jacob[3], Martin[2], Jacob[1]], son of Irvin Gingrich and Vara May (Hunsicker) Ebersole, was born July 21, 1920 at Cleona, Lebanon County, Pa. H died March 20, 1995 at Lebanon, Lebanon County, Pa. and is buried at the cemetery of the Midway Church of the Brethren in South Lebanon Township, Lebanon County, Pa.

On February 27, 1944, he was married to Lorraine L. Mohn at Lebanon, Pa. Lorraine, the daughter of Roy and Elizabeth Lillian (Behney) Mohn, was born December 3, 1922. Lorraine died June 30, 1994. she is buried in the cemetery of the Midway Church of the Brethren.

Issue:

i. Diane Marie , b. September 19,1947. Diane was

married to William Walter Cave June 10, 1967 at Annville, Lebanon County, Pa. William was born March 6, 1943 at Hershey, Dauphin County, Pa.,son of Frank and Miriam (Cocklin) Cave.

    ii. Sharon Louise, b. May 19, 1951 at Lebanon, Pa.

    iii. Randall Irvin, b. September 17, 1954 at Lebanon, Pa.

References:

Gordon, John D., *The Family of Jacob and Kate Ebersole*

Lebanon county, Pa. Orphans Court, Marriage License docket, Vol. 45,
    p. 636

Lebanon Daily News, Lebanon, Pa., March 20, 1995

131. IRENE MAE EBERSOLE [Irvin G.[7,] Cora G.[6] Jacob E.[5], Daniel[4], Jacob[3], Martin[2], Jacob[1]], daughter of Irvin G. and Vara M. (JHunsicker) Ebersole, was born August 16, 1924 at Cleona, Lebanon County, Pa.

Irene was married September 4, 1954 at Manheim, Lancaster County, Pa. to Robert William Kelly, son of Charles Oster and Mary Montgomery (Kugle) Kelly. Robert , a veteran of World War II, died April 1, 1958 and is buried at the cemetery of the East Fairview Church of the Brethren, Manheim, Lancaster county, Pa.

    Issue:

      i. Gail May Kelly, b. September 22, 1955 at Lancaster, Lancaster County, Pa.

      ii. Mark William, b. July 7, 1957 at Lancaster, Pa. and is buried at the East Fairview Church of the Brethren Cemetery, Manheim, Pa.

    References:

Gordon, John D., *The Family of Jacob and Kate Ebersole*

132. ELMER HENRY EBERSOLE [Ammon G.[6], Jacob E.[5], Daniel[4], Jacob[3], Martin[2], Jacob[1]], son of Ammon G. and Amanda (Horst) Ebersole, was born August 12, 1909 in South Annville Township, Lebanon County, Pa.

Elmer married Elizabeth Sauder January 1, 1934 in Epphrata township, Lancaster County, Pa. Elisabeth, the daughter of Amos and Anna (Hoover) Sauder, was born January 25, 1910 in West Earl Township, Lancaster County, Pa.

Elmer died May 4, 1997 at Ephrata, Lancaster County, Pa. His wife died February 26, 1992. Both are buried in Myerstown Mennonite Church Cemetery at Myerstown, Lebanon County, Pa.

Issue:

    i. Elnora who married Ivan Charles Diem on October 1, 1955 at Royer'sMeeting House near Myerstown, Lebanon County, Pa. Ivan was born September 3, 1936 in West Earl Township, Lancaster County, Pa., son of Clarence Irvin and Esther (Horst) Diem

    ii. Elta Sauder, b. January 20, 1938 in West Cocalico Township, Lancaster County, Pa.

    iii Elvin Sauder, b. March 25, 1942 near Lititz, Lancaster County, Pa. On October 26,1963, Elvin was married to Sylvia H. Gingrich in Krall's Mennonite Meeting House, near Schaefferstown, Lebanon County, Pa.

    iv. Wilmer Eugene, b. June 27, 1945 at Lititz, Pa. Wilmer was married November 27, 1965 at Krall's Mennonite Meeting House, near Schaeffertown,Pa.

References:

Gordon, John D., *The Family of Jacob and Kate Ebersole*
Lebanon Daily News, Lebanon, Pa., May 5, 1997

133. KATHRYN ESTHER EBERSOLE [Ammon G.[6], Jacob E.[5], Daniel[4], Jacob[3], Martin[2], Jacob[1]], daughter of Ammon g. and Amanda (Horst) Ebersole, was born April 21, 1911 in North Annville Township, Lebanon, Pa.   Kathryn married Chester Hoover Hershey June 1, 1956. Chester was born August 29, 1892. He died April 22, 1973 and is buried at Hershey's Mennonite Cemetery, Lancaster, Lancaster County, Pa.

Issue:

    i. Landis E. b. November 2,1913. Landis was a step-son

After the death of Chester Kathryn married Albert Allen Hornbberger on December 24, 1976. Albert, son of Martin C. and Kathryn (Nagle) Hornberger, was born March 26,1909. Albert died July 10, 1989 and is buried in Metzler's Mennonite Cemetery, Lancaster County, Pa.

Issue:

    ii. Albert e. b. August 6, 1930. Albert was a ste-son
    iii. John David, b. July 6, 1932. John was a step-son

iv. Landis E., b. August 29 - -. Lanids was a step-son.

On December 8,1990 Kathryn married a third time to Ralph K. Mohler who was born December 17, 1904.

References:

Gordon, John D., *The Jacob and Kate Ebersole F*

134. RUTH ELIZABETH EBERSOLE [Ammon G.[6], Jacob E.[5], Daniel[4], Jacob[3], Martin[2], Jacob[1]], daughter of Ammon g. and Amanda (Horst) Ebersole, was born August 22, 1912 in North Cornwall Township, Lebanon County, Pa.

Ruth was married October 5, 1932 to Joseph Wayne Boll at Mt. Joy, Lancaster county, Pa. Joseph, the son of Joseph A. and Martha (Oberholtzer) Boll, was born September 14, 1912 in Penn Township, Lancaster County, Pa. Joseph died December 30, 1993 and is buried in Erb's Mennonite Cemetery, Lancaster County, Pa.

Joseph Boll was a farmer and an ordained preacher in the Mennonite church. He was ordained June 3, 1947 and preached until 1990.

Issue:

      i. Joseph Richard, b. October 14, 1933
      ii. Orpha ruth, b. August 15, 1935
      iii. Mervin Edward, b.
      iv. Daniel Leon, b. December 7, 1938
      v. Miriam Elizabeth, b. June 16, 1940 in Lancaster County, Pa.
      vi. Mary Jane, b. November 11, 1944 in Lancaster County, Pa.
      vii. Alta Mae Boll, b. January 5, 1947

References:

Gordon, John D., *The Jacob and Kate Ebersole Family*

135. AMMON JACOB EBERSOLE [Ammon G.[6], Jacob E.[5], Daniel[4], Jacob[3], Martin[2], Jacob[1]], son of Ammon G. and Amanda (Horst) Ebersole, was born in Lebanon County, Pa. He died November 5, 1986 at New bunker Hill, Lebanon County, , Pa. and is buried at the Grand View Memorial Park, North Annville Township, Lebanon County, Pa.

Ammon married Vesta Mary Landis on March 26, 1938. Vesta, the daughter of Abram and Mabel (Wanner) Landis, was born July 9, 1919 in Lancaster County, Pa.

Issue:

    i. Kevin Glen M., b. February 19, 1940 at Lebanon, Lebanon County, Pa.

    ii. Mary Suzanne, ,b. July 15, 1941 in North Annville Township, Lebanon County, Pa.

    iii. Doris R., b. September 10, 1945 in Swatara Township, Lebanon County, Pa.

References:
Gordon, john D., *The Jacob and Kate Ebersole Family*
Lebanon Daily News, Lebanon, Pa., November 6, 1986

136. MARTHA MAY EBERSOLE [Ammon G.[6], Jacob E.[5], Daniel[4], Jacob[3], Martin[2], Jacob[1]], daughter of Ammon G. and Amanda (Horst) Ebersole, was born September 10, 1916 in North Annville Township, Lebanon County, Pa.

Martha Nay was married to Charles Francis Walter at Campbelltown, Lebanon County, Pa. Charles, the son of Ira and Rebecca (Dundore) Waiter, was born June 20, 1917 at Buffalo Springs, Lebanon County, Pa.

Issue:

    i. Nancy Marie, b. December 7, 1946; m. September to Richard Adair Starr

    ii. Anita Rebecca, b. January 8, 1948 at Buffalo Springs; m. December 23, 1977 at Myerstown, Lebanon County, Pa.

    iii. Stanley Kenneth Walter, b. April 6, 1949 in Buffalo Springs; m. June 1, 1974 to Cinthia Nauman

References:
Gordon ,John D., *The Jacob and Kate Ebersole Family*

137. AARON HAROLD EBERSOLE [Ammon G.[6], Jacob E.[5], Daniel[4], Jacob[3], Martin[2], Jacob[1]], son of Ammon G. and Amanda (horst) Ebersole, was born April 1, 1921 in North Annville Township, Lebanon County, Pa.

On August 19, 1950, Aaron married Ruth Marie Ober at Hernley's Mennonite Church in Rapho Township, Lancaster County, Pa. Ruth, the daughter of Elmer M. and Minnie (Johnson) Ober, was born August 19, 1925 in Rapho Township, Lancaster County, Pa.

Aaron was a farmer.

Issue:

  i. Marie Jane, b. January 25, 1953 at Lebanon, Lebanon county, Pa.

  ii. John Harold, b. February 1, 1954 near Myerstown, Lebanon County, Pa.

  iii. Linda May, b. May 27, 1960 near Myerstown

References:

Gordon, John D., *The Family of Jacob and Kate Ebersole*

138. PAUL HERMAN EBERSOLE [Ammon G.[6], Jacob E.[5], Daniel[4], Jacob[3], Martin[2], Jacob[1]], son of Ammon G. and Amanda (Horst) Ebersole, was born November 29, 1918 in North Annville Township, Lebanon County, Pa.

On July 31, 1943 Paul was married to Luella H. Risser in the home of the bride at Brunnerville, Lancaster County, Pa. Luella, the daughter of Christ S. and Anna W. (Hernley) Risser, was born December 16, 1919 Brunnerville.

Issue:

  i. Mark, b. April 5, 1948 in Sooth Annville Township.

References:

Gordon, John D., *The Family of Jacob and Kate Ebersole*

 Lebanon County, Pa.

On June 6, 1964, Cora was married to Carl R. Gerber at Fairmount, Belmont County, Ohio. Carl, son of Peter J. and Anna J. (Hostetter) Gerber, was born March 5, 1907. He died September 24, 1987 at Kidron, Ohio

139. NORMAN JOSEPH EBERSOLE [Ammon G.[6], Jacob E.[5], Daniel[4], Jacob[3], Martin[2], Jacob[1]], son of Ammon G. and Amanda (Horst) Ebersole, was born July 13, 1928 in North Annville Township, Lebanon County, Pa.

On October 26, 1946 Norma married June Caroline Wine in Gingrich's Mennonite Church, North Cornwall township, Lebanon County, Pa. June, the daughter of George E. and Hazel (Heatwole) Wine, was born October 17, 1925 in Hyatville, Md.

Issue:

  i. Nelson Leroy, b. October 19, 1947 at Manheim, Rapho Township, Lancaster County, Pa.

  ii. Nathan Leonard, b. May 7, 1949 at Lebanon, Lebanon County, Pa.

iii. Nevin Lester, b. October 21, 1950 at Palmyra, Lebanon County, Pa.

iv. Neil Leslie, b. February 7, 1953 in West Cornwall Township, Lebanon County, Pa.

v. Dianne Louise, b. November 23, 1955 at Lebanon, LebanonCounty, Pa.

vi. Norman Lynn, b. February 10, 1958 at Lebanon, Pa.

References:

Gordon, John D., *The Family of Jacob and Kate Ebersole*

140. JOHN DAVID GORDON [Edna[6], Jacob E.[5], Daniel[4], Jacob[3], Martin[2], Jacob[1]], son of John M. and Edna (Ebersole) Gordon, was born December 7, 1925 at Hershey, Derry Township, Dauphin County, Pa.

On October 15, 1949 John was married to Esther Elaine "Dolly" Jamison at Hanoverdale, Dauphin County, Pa. Esther was born October 12, 1929 at Campbelltown, Lebanon county, Pa., the daughter of Charles Elmer and Emma Florence (Eckert) Jamison.

Issue:

153.   i. Edward Alan, b. February 9, 1951 at Hershey, Dauphin County, Pa.

References::

Gordon, John d., *The Family of Jacob and Kate Ebersole*

Lebanon County, Pa. Orphans Court, Marriage License docket, Vol. 51, p. 1385

141. ROBERT ARTHUR HEILMAN [F. Irene[7], Clinton[6], Elias A.[5]. John M;[4], Jacob B.[3], John[2], Jacob[1]], son of Arthur S. and F. Irene (Ebersole) Heilman was born October 13, 1920 at Lebanon, LebanonCounty, Pa.

On April 26, 1945, Robert was married to Josephine Janet Zehring at Brownwood, Brown County, Texas. Josephine, the daughter of Ella E. Barr and adopted daughter of William H. Zehring, was born May 5, 1921 at Annville, LebanonCounty, Pa.

during World War II, Robert served with U. S. Army in Alaska and the Aleutian Islands. He was awarded a bronze battle star for participation in the battle of Attu.

Josephine, also served in the military during World War II. She was a lieutenant in the U. S. Army Nurse Corps stationed at camp Bowie in Texas.

Issue:

151.	i. Robert, Arthur Jr., b. May 9, 1946
152.	ii. John Peter, b. June 1,1951
	iii. James Joseph, b. January 12, 1956

References
Heilman, Robert A.,Personal knowledge

142. NANCY JANICE HEILMAN [F. Irene[7], Clinton[6], Elias A.[5]. John M;[4], Jacob B.[3], John[2], Jacob[1]], daughter of Arthur S. and F. Irene (Ebersole) Heilman, was born October 23, 1928 at Lebanon, Lebanon County, Pa.

Nancy was married Harold Alvin Kadle on February 5. 1949 by the Rev. Pierce E. Swope at Lebanon, Pa. Harold, son of Horace P. and Elsie (Cordell) Kadle was born My 8, 1925 at Mercersburg, Frankl;in County, Pa. He died December 1, 1956 at Brooklyn, New York and is buried at the Grand View Memorial Park, Annville, Lebanon County, Pa.

After the death of Harold, Nancy was married to Richard Allen White on August 10, 1957 by the Rev. Ralph D. Althouse at Lebanon, Pa. Richard, the son of Harry L. and Ella (Stohler) White, was born June 29, 1932.

Richard is a CPA. Nancy and her family live at Cleona, Lebanon, Pa.

Issue:

    i. Heidi Ann, a daughter by adoption. Heidi Ann was born November 15, 1958. She was married twice. Her first husband was John Sims with whom she had a son, Jared. Her second husband is William Hartzell with whom she has a son, Brian.

References:
Heilman, Robert A., Personal knowledge
Records of Tabor Reformed Church (now UCC, Lebanon, Pa.
White, Nancy J., Personal interview

143. RUTH E. CARPER [Ella M.[7], Allen L.6, Elias A.[5], John[4], Jacob.[3], John[2], Jacob[1]], daughter of Frank S. and Ella M.(Ebersole) Carper, was born December 5, 1917 at Palmyra, Lebanon County, Pa. She died at Harrisburg, Dauphin County, Pa. on August 10, 1981 and is buried at the Spring Creek Cemetery, Hershey, Dauphin County, Pa.

On June 3, 1939, Ruth was married to the Rev. J. Herbert Miller at Palmyra, Pa. by her father, the Rev. Frank S. .Carper. J. Herbert, the son of Jesse H. and Louise (Rinehart) Miller, was born in 1916 at Baltimore, Md.

Like his father-in=law, he was an ordained minister in the Church of the

Brethren. The Rev. Miller was the pastor of the Spring Creek Church of the Brethren at Hershey, Pa. until his death on March 8, 1979. The Rev. Miller was buried with his wife at the Spring Creek Cemetery, Hershey, Pa.

Ruth was an elementary school teacher in the Hershey schools and also in the Ebenezer school district in North Lebanon Township, Lebanon County, Pa.

ruth and her family lived at Palmyra, Pa.

Issue:

        i. David P., b.
        ii. Robert C., b.
        iii. John H., b.

References:

Gravestone inscriptions, Spring Creek Cemetery, Hershey, Pa.

Lebanon County, Pa. Orphans Court, Marriage License Docket, Vol. 25,
     p. 539

Lebanon Daily News, Lebanon, Pa.,August 11, 1981

144. MIRIAM NAOMI CARPER [Ella M.[7], Allen L.6, Elias A.[5], John[4], Jacob.[3] , John[2], Jacob[1]], daughter of Frank S. and Ella M. (Ebersole) Carper,, was born about 1928.

Miriam was married to Kenneth Frey on June 1, 1944. Kenneth, the son of Paul R. and Carrie May (Frederick) Frey, was born in 1922 at Elizabthtown, Lancaster County, Pa.

Kenneth was a bookkeeper and Miriam was a music supervisor.

The Freys made their home t Palmyra, Pa.

Issue:

        i. Jeffrey Carper, b. April 5, 1951

References:

Carper, F. S., *History of the Palmyra Church of the Brethren 1892-1967,*
     p. 293 Printed by Forry and Hacker, Lancaster, Pa.

145.. JOHN MARK CARPER [Ella M.[7], Allen L.6, Elias A.[5], John[4], Jacob.[3] , John[2], Jacob[1]], son of Frank S. and Ella M. (Ebersole)Carper, was born May 2, 1926 at Palmyra, Lebanon County, Pa.

On June 26, 1948, John was married to Jane Reidenbough at Palmyra, Pa. by the Rev. Frank S. Carper, father of the groom.

John Mark carper was a pediatrician at Lancaster, Pa. and later at Wellesley, Massachusetts.. He may have been married a second time to Iris whose surname is not known.

Issue: (all born in Lebanon County, Pa.)

     i. Joseph Michael, b. April 25, 1951

     ii. Ann Elisabeth, b. November 2, 1954

     iii. James David, b. April 15, 1956

References:

Carper, F. S., *History of the Palmyra Church of the Brethren 1892-1967,*
    pp. 293, 295, 297 Printed by Forry and Hacker, Lancaster, Pa.

146. GERALD R. EBERSOLE [Harry M.[7], Allen L.[6], Elias A.[5],
John[4], Jacob.[3] , John[2], Jacob[1]], son of Harry M. and Bernice (Myers)
Ebersole, was born July 13, 1934 at Hershey, Dauphin County, Pa.

    Gerald was married to Ruth Ann Longenecler on September 22, 1956 at
Palmyra, Lebanon County, Pa. Ruth ann, the daughter of Robert N. and
Beatrice (Wilhelm) Longenecker, was born August 27, 1956 at Hershey, Pa.

    Both Gerald and Ruth are public school teachers.

Issue:

     i. James Gerald, b. January 9, 1961

     ii. Steven william, b. May 15, 1963

References:

Carper, F. S., *History of the Palmyra Chinch of the Brethren 18892-1967,*
    pp. , 286, , 302 Printed by Forry and Hacker, Lancaster, Pa.

147. RUSSELL C. KEEFER [Charles E.[7],. Elizabeth[6], Elias A.[5],
John[4], Jacob.[3] , John[2], Jacob[1]], son of Charles e. and Mabel J. (Herr)
Keefer, was born January 19, 1920 at Lebanon, Lebanon County, Pa.

    Russell was married at Frederick, Md. to Ruth Louise Louser December
12, 1941. Ruth Louise, the daughter of Herman and Marion (Raush) Loser,
was born December 9, 1922 at Lebanon, Pa.

    Russell succeeded his father as head of the Lebanon Hardware Co. a
company in which he and his wife, Ruth Louise, were the principal
stockholders.

Issue:

154.   i. David Russell, b. December 15, 1942

     ii. Diane Louise, b. July 29, 1945. Diane was married to
        William Henry Troutman on February 11, 1973 at
        Fredericksburg, Lebanon County, Pa. William, the son
        of Henry G. and Edith (Groff) Troutman, was born

September 20, 1946 at Fredericksburg, Pa. After a number of years the marriage was terminated by divorce.

References:

Keefer, Personal interview

Lebanon County, Pa. Orphans Court, Marriage License Docket, Vol. 66, p. 446

ibid., vol. 74, p.138

148. ROY A. KEEFER [Grant[7], Elizabeth[6], Elias A.[5], John[4], Jacob.[3], John[2], Jacob[1]], son of Grant E. and Lizzie)Eisenhauer) Keefer, was born February 11, 1923 in North Annville township, Lebanon County, Pa. He died April 25, 2003 at Berkshire Center, Exeter Township, Berks County, Pa.

Roy was married to Mary E. Stohler of whom nothing more is known.

He served in the U. S. Army during World War II. After the war he was employed by UAG of Robesonia, Berks County, Pa.

Issue:

> i. Michael Lee, b. September 1956 at Lebanon, Lebanon County, Pa. Michael was married to Diana Louisa Walmer on June 15, 1980 at Annville, Lebanon County, Pa. Diana was born May 27, 1955 at Lebanon, Pa., the daughter of Marvin M. and Carrie M. (Frantz) Walmer.
>
> ii. Patrick L., b.
>
> iii. Judith Ann, b. April 4, 1940 at Lebanon, Pa. Judith was married March 25, 19-- to Edward Michael Wagner at Lebanon, Pa. Edward, the son of George and Della (Firestone) Wagner, was born July 24, 1949 at Lebanon,Pa.

References:

Keefer, Russell C., Personal interview

Lebanon County, Pa. Orphans Court, Marriage License Docket, Vol. 72, p. 787

Ibid.., Vol. 83, p.236

149. JAMES JARED HORN JR. [Pearl[7], Susan P.[5], Elias A.[5], John[4], Jacob.[3], John[2], Jacob[1]], son of James Jared and Pearl S. (Sellers) Horn, was born November 13, 1926 at Annville, Lebanon County, Pa. He died

February 7, 1983 and is buried at the Mt. Annville Cemetery, Annville, Pa.

Jared, the mame by which he was best known was married Dorothy Speraw, the daughter of Walter E. and Violet (Basehore) Speraw, on February 28, 1948. Dorothy was born in 1928.

Jared was one of the first ,if not the first, in Lebanon County to offer the public "fast food" when he opened his restaurant known as *Super 15.* Jared's restaurant was located at the west end of Cleona.

Issue: (both born in Lebanon County, Pa.)

    i. Lois Marie, b. September 13, 1948 at Lebanon, Pa. Lois was married March 21, 1969 to John Richard Hazleton. John, the son of S. Richard and Andrea (Haag) Hazleton,was born September 8, 1946.

    ii. Sharon Jean, b. July 22,1950 at Lebanon, Pa. Sharon married John Riganati on July 22,1989 at Lebanon. John, the son of Rocco and Rita (Grillo) Riganati, was born December 14, 1930 Brooklyn, New York.

After the death of Jared, Dorothy married William Haak, one time co-owner of Haaks Department Store at Lebanon.

References:

Horn, David, Persona interview

Lebanon County, Pa. Orphans Court, Marriage License Docket, Vol. 49, p. 711

ibid., Vol. 69, p. 401

" Vol. 101, p. 6 26

150. DAVID HORN [Pearl[7], Susan P.[5], Elias A.[5], John[4], Jacob.[3], John[2], Jacob[1]], son of James Jared and Pearl S. (Sellers) Horn, was born December 14, 1929 at Annville, Lebanon County, Pa.

David was married to Doris J. Behm May 9, 1952 at Annville, Pa. Doris, the daughter of Howard R. and Rosanna (Gebhart) Behm, was born December 29, 1930 at Annville, Pa.

David was a printer . His wife was a bookkeeper. David and his family live at Annville, Pa.

Issue: (all born in Lebanon County, Pa.)

    i. Kathleen Louise, b. October 22, 1953 at Lebanon, Pa. Kathleen married William Patrick Tice on May 13, 1971 at Annville, Lebanon County, Pa. William, son of John and Mary (Showers) Tice,was born March 26, 1953 at

Lebanon, Pa. William was a pattern maker and Kathleen was a student at the time of their marriage.

ii Loretta, b. September 5, 1956. Loretta married William Fertes.

iii. Daniel, b. July 5, 1976. Daniel married Debbie Chisholm. That marriage ended in divorce. On August 6, 1988, Daniel was married to Pamela Susan Smith at Annville, Pa. Pamela, daughter of Clarence Naggle and Catharine Mary (Molesevich) Smith, was born July 13, 1959 at Lebanon, Pa. At the time of their marriage, Daniel was a railroad signalman and his wife was a machine operator.

References:

Horn, David, Personal interview
Lebanon County, Pa. Orphans Court, Marriage License Docket,
    Vol. 54, p. 15
Ibid., Vol. 72, p. 38
 "   Vol. 99, p. 97

151. ROBERT A. HEILMAN, JR. [Robert A.8, F. Irene7, Clinton6, Elias A.5. John M;4, Jacob B.3, John2, Jacob1], son of Robert A. and Josephine J. (Zehring) Heilman, was born May 9, 1946 at Lebanon, Lebanon County, Pa.

On June 1972, he married Kathleen Braun Clark, daughter of John and Catharine (Fraytic) Braun, Jr. at Lebanon, Pa. kathleen was born October 14, 1947 at Lebanon, Pa. Kathleen had been married previously to Thomas Clark from whom she was divorced.

Robert was employed by General Public Utilities at Three Mile Island as a nuclear operator until his retirement.

Robert and his family live near Hummelstown, Dauphin County, Pa.

Issue:

i. Renee, b. August 8, 1968 at Lebanon, Pa. Renee was born a Clark but was adopted by Robert. She was married to Steve Buck, a native of Delaware, on June 25, 2005 at Hershey, Dauphin County, Pa.

155.. ii. Jennifer Lee, b. December 13, 1972 at Camp Hill, Cumberland County, Pa.

References:

Heilman, Robert A., Personal knowledge
Lebanon County, Pa. Orphans Court, Marriage License Docket, Vol. 73, p. 269
Lebanon Daily News, Lebanon, Pa., September 6, 1967
Records of Tabor Reformed Chinch (now UCC), Lebanon, Pa.

152. JOHN PETER HEILMAN [Robert A.8, F. Irene7, Clinton6, Elias A.5. John M;4, Jacob B.3, John2, Jacob1], son of Robert A. and Josephine J. (Zehring) Heilman, was born June 1, 1951 at Lebanon, Lebanon County, Pa.

On June 21, 1973, John was married to Susan Brehm Espinosa at San Bernardin0, California. Susan, daughter of Harry J. and Mae E. (White) Brehm was born January 9, 1950. Susan had three children from a previous marriage. They are: Robin, Robert and Amanda Espinosa.

John is retired from the U. S. Air Force and is employed by the U. S. Postal Service at Nashville, Tennessee He and his family live at Ashland City, TN.

References:
Heilman, John Peter, Personal interview
Heilman, Robert A, Personal knowledge
Records, Tabor Reformed Church *now UCC), Lebanon, Pa.

153. EDWARD ALAN GORDON [John D7, Edna6, Jacob E.5, Daniel4, Jacob3, Martin2, Jacob1], son of John D. and Esther (Jamison) Gordon, was born February 9, 1951 at Hershey, Dauphin County, Pa.

Edward was married July 13, 1974 to Barbara Marie Bavington at Paxtang,, Dauphin county, Pa. Barbara, daughter of W. Wayne and Marie Cecelia (m (Myhre(,Bavington, Jr., was born April 6, 1952 at Harrisburg, Dauphin County, Pa.

Edward is an elementary school teacher at Ephrata, Lancaster County, Pa. Barbara is a school teacher in the Elizabthtown school district.

Issue: (Both born at Harrisburg, Dauphin County, Pa.)
    i. John David II, b. September 8. 1980
    ii. Amy Jo, b. February 8, 1984

Referee:
Gordon, John d., The Family of Jacob and Kate Ebersole

.154. DAVID RUSSELL KEEFER [Russell C.,8 Charles E.7,. Elizabeth6, Elias A.5, John4, Jacob.3, John2, Jacob1], son of Russell C. and

ruth Louise (Louser) Keefer, was born December 15, 1942 at Lebanon, Lebanon County, Pa.

David was married to Mildred Carol Engel on June 18, 1966 at Lebanon, Pa. Mildred, the daughter of Frank and Mildred E. (Helms) Engel, was born on July 22, 1948 at Lebanon, Pa.

David'soccupationatthe time of marriage was that of an electrician. Mildred was student.

Issue:

> i. Amy Jane, b. January 29, 1975 at Hershey, Dauphin County, Pa. She was married to Randall Schreffler July 22,2000 at Grantham, Pa.

References:
Keefer, Russell C., Personal interview
Lebanon County, Pa. Orphans Court, Marriage License Docket,
    Vol.66, p. 446

155. JENNIFER LEE HEILMAN [Robert A. Jr.,,[9] Robert A.[8], F. Irene[7], Clinton[6], Elias A.[5]. John M;[4], Jacob B.[3] , John[2], Jacob[1]], daughter of Robert A. and Kathleen (Clark) Heilman, Jr., was born December 13, 1972 at Camp Hill, Cumberland County, Pa.

Jennifer was married to Christopher Michael bushman on May 27, 1990 by the Mayor of Hummelstown, Pa., Marion Alexander, at Hershey, Dauphin C County, Pa. Christopher, son of Paul W. and Donna Jean (Shaffer) bushman, was born February 19, 1971 at Lebanon, Lebanon County, Pa.

Jennifer and her family live at Plymouth circle, Hershey, Pa. Both she and her husband are employed by the MILTON S. Hershey Medical Center at Hershey, Pa.

Issue:

> i. A daughter, Zoe, ey adoption.Zoe was born February 19, 2004 in China.

Bushman, Jennifer, Personal interview
Heilman, Robert A., Personal knowledge

Index

Brenneman, Henry 8
Buck, Steve 105
Burkey, Fred N. 44
Burkholder, Abraham 21
Burkholder, Benjamin 13
Burkholder, Elizabeth Whisler 21
Burkholder, John 20
Burkholder, Lizzie E. 21
Burkholder, Mary Martin 13
Burkholder, Samuel 13, 25
Burkholder, Susanna 21
Bushman, Christopher Michael 107
Bushman, Donna Jean 107
Bushman, PaulW. 107
Byers, John J. 46
Byers, John J. Jr. 46
Byers, Noah E. 46
Carper, Allen B.84
Carper, Ann E;ozabeth 101
Carper, Fannie Stauffer 84
Carper, Frank Stauffer 84
Carper, James David 101
Carper, John M. 85
Carper, John Michael 101
Carper, Joseph Michael 101
Carper, Miriam Naomi 85, 101
Carper, Ruth E. 84, 100
Cave, Frank 93
Cave, Miriam Cocklin 93
Cave, William Walter 93
Chisholm, Debbie 104
Clark, Kathleen Braun 105
Conrad, David 50
Daumler, Anna 4
Demler, Henry 30
Detweiler, Annie Burkey 48
Diem, Clarence Irvin 94
Diem, Esther Horst 94

Diem, Ivan Charles 94
Dietz,Minnie 53
Diffenderfer, Sarah 26
Dohner, W. H. 35
Ebersol, Christian 77
Ebersol, Mary 77
Ebersole, Aaron Harold 81, 97
Ebersole, Aaron S. 10, 62
Ebersole, Abner Longenecker 73
Ebersole, Abraham 10, 19, 25
Ebersole, Abraham B. 6
Ebersole, Abraham Burkholder 19
Ebersole, Abraham E. 31, 64
Ebersole, Abraham H. 52
Ebersole, Abraham L. 19, 29
Ebersole, Ada 31, 63
Ebersole, Ada Longenecker 73
Ebersole, Adaline 22
Ebersole, Adam Risser 78
Ebersole, Agnes O. 60
Ebersole, Albert S. 63
Ebersole, Allen Longenecker 34, 67
Ebersole, Alma 55
Ebersole, Amanda 22, 27, 56
Ebersole, Amanda K. 58, 62
Ebersole, Amelia D. 26
Ebersole, Ammmon Gingrich 65, 81,
Ebersole, Ammon Jacob 81, 96
Ebersole, Amos 34, 50
Ebersole, Amos A.
Ebersole, Amos D. 26, 54
Ebersole, Amos E. 31, 40, 63
Ebersole, Amos H. 52
Ebersole, Amos N. 51
Ebersole, Amos R. 19, 43, 76
Ebersole, Amos W. 77
Ebersole, Ann 50
Ebersole, Anna 8, 11, 12, 18, 22,

Ebersole, Della Catharine 65
Ebersole, Dianne Louise 98
Ebersole, Diane Marie 93
Ebersole, Dora W. 77
Ebersole, Doris R. 96
Ebersole, Dorothy 75
Ebersole, Edith S. 53
Ebersole, Edith Longenecker 73
Ebersole, Edna Mae 65, 83
Ebersole, Edwin 55
Ebersole, Elam Risser 78
Ebersole, Eleanor Ruth 75
Ebersole, Elias A. 15, 34
Ebersole, Elias B. 21
Ebersole, Elias Rutt 19, 45
Ebersole, Eli D. 26, 53
Ebersole, Elisabeth 10
Ebersole, Elisabeth B. 6
Ebersole, Elizabeth 4, 12, 19, 24, 27, 28, 30, 31, 38, 40, 45, 59, 72,82
Ebersole, Elizabeth A.15, 32
Ebersole, Elizabeth B. 20, 21
Ebersole, Elizabeth Frey 11
Ebersole, Elizabeth gingrich 65
Ebersole, Elizabeth Gish 17, 36
Ebersole, Elizabeth H. 27
Ebersole, Elizabeth K. 7
Ebersole, Elizabeth Longenecker 34, 69
Ebersole, Elizabeth O. 60
Ebersole, Eliza May 48
Ebersole, Ella 44
Ebersole, Ella D 26
Ebersole, Ella M. 67, 84
Ebersole, Ella S. 59
Ebersole, Ella Sauder 94
Ebersole, Ellen 63

Ebersole, Ellen R. 39
Ebersole, Ellen W. 64
Ebersole, Elvin Sauder 94
Ebersole, Emma 43, 56, 61
Ebersole, Emma D. 26
Ebersole, Emma Longenecker 34, 68
Ebersole, Emma O. 60
Ebersole, Emma Verna 83
Ebersole, Elmer Henry 81, 94
Ebersole, Elmer S. 59
Ebersole, Elnora 94
Ebersole, Ephraim 22, 25
Ebersole, Esther 19, 45, 46
Ebersole, Ethel A. 54
Ebersole, Fannie 2, 11, 62
Ebersole, Fannie G. 3
Ebersole, Fannie K. 7
Ebersole, Fannie N. 12
Ebersole, Fannie R. 43,78
Ebersole, Fanny 18, 31, 44
Ebersole, Fanny H. 52
Ebersole, Frank 49, 50, 62
Ebersole, Frank S. 45
Ebersole, Frany 10
Ebersole, Frany Irene 67, 83
Ebersole, George 13, 62
Ebersole, George Monroe 34
Ebersole, Gerald 85
Ebersole, Gerald R.101
Ebersole, Gertrude 54
Ebersole, Gertrude N. 53
Ebersole, Grace A. 70
Ebersole, Grace S. 63
Ebersole, Harold 75
Ebersole, Harold L. 55
Ebersole, Harold Leon 48
Ebersole, Harold W. 71
Ebersole, Harry 75

Ebersole, Harry J. 76
Ebersole, Harry M. 57, 85
Ebersole, Harry R. 3
Ebersole, Harvey 56
Ebersole, Helen M. 54
Ebersole, Henry 12
Ebersole, Henry C. 23
Ebersole, Henry Clinton
Longenecker 34, 66
Ebersole, Henry E. 12
Ebersole, Henry H. 29, 61
Ebersole, Henry K. 8, 23, 24
Ebersole, Henry Moyer 17
Ebersole, Henry R 6
Ebersole, Henry Rutt 11
Ebersole, Henry S. 79
Ebersole, Ida S. 59, 63
Ebersole, Ira Risser 78
Ebersole, Irene Mae 80, 94
Ebersole, Irvin Gingrich 80
Ebersole, Isaac L. 35
Ebersole, Kenneth J. 71
Ebersole, Isaac Longenecker 70
Ebersole, Irvin 55
Ebersole, Irvin Gingrich 65
Ebersole, IrvinPeter 81
Ebersole, Jacob 1, 2, 4, 6, 9, 11, 13, 24
Ebersole, Jacob A. 16, 27, 35
Ebersole, Jacob B. 2
Ebersole, Jacob Bossler 5
Ebersole, Jacob C. 23
Ebersole, Jacob E. 31, 64
Ebersole, Jacob G. 3, 8, 65
Ebersole, Jacob H. 38
Ebersole, Jacob K. 7, 55
Ebersole, Jacob L. 29, 60
Ebersole, Jacob Longenecker 73

Ebersole, Jacob M. 2, 7, 18
Ebersole, Jaocb Moyer 6, 16, 17, 39
Ebersole, Jacob N. 52
Ebersole, Jacob R. 9, 28, 55, 61
Ebersole, Jacob Risser 78
Ebersole, Jacob S. 59
Eberolse, James E. 36
Ebersole, James Gerald 102
Ebersole, Jay Raymond 76
Ebersole, Jennie Detweiler 48
Ebersole, Jennie O. 60
Ebersole, John 1, 3, 4, 5, 12, 13
Ebersole, John A. 15, 33
Ebersole, John B. 2, 41
Ebersole, John D. 26, 55
Ebersole, John David 6, 18
Ebersole, John E. 9, 40
Ebersole, John Frey 11, 29
Ebersole, John Gish 17, 37
Ebersole, John H. 38, 74
Ebersole, JohnHarold 97
Ebersole, John Herman 67
Ebersole, John Irvin 73
Ebersole, John K. 27, 61
Ebersole, John L. 10
Ebersole, John M. 15, 56
Ebersole, John Moyer 6, 14
Ebersole, John R. 3, 8, 10, 18, 26, 43
Ebersole, John S. 59
Ebersole, John W. 42
Ebersole, Johnson O. 60
Ebersole, Jonas Longenecker 34
Ebersole, Jonas W. 77
Ebersole, Joseph 8, 24
Ebersole, Joseph Moyer 17
Ebersole, Joseph N. 25
Ebersole, Joseph R. 27

Ebersole, Neil Leonard 98
Ebersole, Nelson Leroy 98
Ebersole, Nevin Lester 98
Ebersole, Noah 55
Ebersole, Noah N. 24
Ebersole, Nora W. 77
Ebersole, Norman Clayton 76
Ebersole, Morman Joseph 98
Ebersole, Norman Lynn 98
Ebersole, Norman S. 79
Ebersole, Paul 75
Ebersole, Paul Herman 81, 97
Ebersole, Paul I. 42
Ebersole, Peter 25
Ebersole, Peter C. 23, 50
Ebersole, Peter E. 50
Ebersole, Peter K. 27, 57
Ebersole, Peter L. 29, 59
Ebersole, Peter R. 3, 8, 9, 27
Ebersole, Phoebe H. 38, 75
Ebersole, Ralph E. 36
Ebersole, Randall Irvin 93
Ebersole, Ray Henry 49
Ebersole, Raymond 71
Ebersole, Raymond s. 63
Ebersole, Rebecca H. 52
Ebersole, Reuben 45, 55, 62
Ebersole, Reuben O. 60
Ebersole, Roy Irvin 83
Ebersole, Russell H. 75
Ebersole, Ruth 62, 75
Ebersole, Ruth Elizabeth 81, 95
Ebersole, Ruth Longenecker 73
Ebersole, Sabina 19, 47
Ebersole, Sadie 36, 57, 71
Ebersole, Sally W. 64
Ebersole, Samuel 23, 27, 62
Ebersole, Samuel B. 21

Ebersole, Samuel D. 6, 21
Ebersole, Samuel E. 31
Ebersole, Samuel H. 24
Ebersole, Samuel M.56
Ebersole, Samuel Moyer 17, 39
Ebersole, Samuel W. 3, 12, 31
Ebersole, Sara O. 60
Ebersole, Sarah 24, 31, 55
Ebersole, Sarah A. 15
Ebersole, Sarah Ann 10
Ebersole, Sarah Lizzie 32
Ebersole, sarah Shenk 31
Ebersole, S. Earl 53
Ebersole, Seth E. 50, 79
Ebersole, Sharon Louise 93
Ebersole, Solomon D. 26
Ebersole, Solomon R. 8, 19, 25, 26
Ebersole, Solomon W. 53
Ebersole, Stella Blanche 49
Ebersole, Steven william102
Ebersole, Susan 50
Ebersole, Susan Longenecker 73
Ebersole, Susan P. 35, 69
Ebersole, Susanna 13, 30
Ebersole, Susanna B. 21
Ebersoloe,Susanna H. 38,74
Ebersole, Susie E. 56
Ebersole, Tillman 60
Ebersole, Tillman R. 43
Ebersole, Veronica 2, 8, 27
Rbersole, Veronica R. 9
Ebersole, Viola 71
Ebersole, Viola Esther 65
Ebersole, William C. 45
Ebersole, Wilmer Eugene 95
Ebersoll, Frances 1
Ebersoll, Jacob 1
Eby, Mary B. 50

Gordon, John David 83, 98
Gordon, John David Jr. 106
Gordon, McKinley 83
Grelberis, Edward 93
Greenly, John C. 56
Groff, Amanda Conrad 70
Groff, Christian C. 86
Groff, Hilda J.87
Groff, John 70
Groff, John H, 56
Groff, Jonas B. 73
Groff, LeRoy 86
Groff, Minerva G. 70
Groff, Naomi 87
Groff, Phares B. 73
Groff, Susan Baker 73
Gruber, ISabella E. 39
Gruber, Jacob 21
Gruber, Lizzie 42
Haak, William 103
Hackman, Willis 16
Hartzell, Brian 100
Hartzell, Richard 100
Hatton, Sylvanus 37
Hayworth, Lyn 91
Hazleton, Andrea Haas 103
Hazleton, John Richard 103
Hazleton, S. Richard 103
Heilman, Arthur Stine 84
Heilman, Grant 84
Heilman, James Joseph 99
Heilman, Jennifer Lee 105, 106
Heilman, John Peter 99, 105
Heilman, Mariah Stine 84
Heilman, Nancy Janice 84, 99
Heilman, Renee 105
Heilman, Robert Arthur 84, 99
Heilman, Robert Arthur Jr. 99, 106

Heisey, Ira 61
Heisey, John S. 41
Heisey, Lizzie Gibble 61
Heisey, Samuel L. 61
Heistand, Katherine B. 61
Heller, Bertha 40
Heller, Fanny Rohrer 40
Heller, Henry L. 40
Henry, Levi L. 30
Herchilroth, Elizabeth 14
Hernley, Anna W. Risser 98
Hernley, Charles 97
Hernley, Mary 20
Herr, David 89
Herr, Fannie Brandt 89
Herr, Michael 89
Hershey, Chester Hoover 95
Hershey, Landis E. 95
Hershey, Lizzie 20
Hertzler, Alta Burkhart 73
Hertzler, Daniel Zimmerman 91
Hertzler, Ella Miller 91
Hertzler, Emma M. 73
Hertzler, Mabel 91
Hertzler, Owen A. 73
Hess, Clayton M. 59
Hill, A. P.36
Hill, Nell 36
Hoffer, Christ H. 73
Hoffer, Maggie Greiiner 73
Hoffer, Mildred E. 773
Hoffman, John 2,
Honafius, George 38
Honafius, Harriet Lowery 38
Honafius, Phhilip 38
Horn, David 90, 104
Horn, Elizabeth H. Steely 90
Horn, James Jared 90, 103

Horn, James Jared Jr.90
Horn, Joseph 90
Horn, Kathleen Louise 104
Horn, Lois Marie 103
Horn, Loretta 104
Horn, Philip 90
Horn, Sharon Jean 103
Hornberger, Albert Allen 95
Hornberger, Allen E. 95
Hornberger, John David 95
Hornberger, Kathry Nagle 95
Hornberger, Landis E.95
Hornberger, Martin C. 95
Horning, Leah 46
Horst, Amanda Gingrich 81
Horst, Nancy 29
Horst, Peter 81
Hunsicker, Frank 80
Hunsicker, Lizzie Zimmerman 80
Hunsicker, Vara May 80
Jamison, Charles Elmer 99
Jamison, EmmaEmma Florence 99
Jamison, Esther Elaine 98
Kadle, Elsie Cordell 99
Kadle, Harold Alvin 99
Kadle, HoraceD.99
Kauffman, Barbara 7, 13
Kauffman, John Moyer 13
Keefer, Amy Jane 106
Keefer, Charles E. 89
Keefer, David Russell 102, 106
Keefer, Diane Louise 102
Keefer, Grant E. 89
Keefer, Judith Ann 103
Keefer, MichaelLee 103
Keefer, Roy A. 89, 102
Keefer, Russell C.89, 102
Keefer, Susan Ebersole 87

Keenports, Lydia 18, 39
Kelly, Charles Oster 94
Kelly, Gail May 94
Kelly, Mark William 94
Kelly, Mary Montgomery Kugle 94
Kelly,Robert William 94
Kendig, Susan 27
Kennedy, Loyd H. 54
Kiefer, Anna 69
Kiefer, Anna S. 70
Kiefer, Clarence E. 69, 88
Kiefer, Charles E. 69, 88
Kiefer, Grant E. 69
Kiefer, Jeremiah 69
Kiefer, John Adam 69
Kiefer, Katherine 69
Kiefer, Susan E. 69
King, Monroe 57
Koser, Abner A. 76
Koser, Paris 76
Koser, Vivian 76
Kraybill, Nancy 25
Kreider, Abraham E. 46
Kreider, Amos E. 46
Kreider, Annie 65
Kreider, Frank E. 46
Kreider, Henry E. 46
Kreider, John 46
Kreider, John e. 46
Kreider, Lizzie 49
Kreider, Matilda 46
Kreider, Moses 65
Kreider, Sarah Bomberger 65
Kreiner, Ezra E. 72
Kreiner, Fred W. 72
Kreiner, John E. 72
Kreiner, Mary 72
Kreiner, W. F. 72

Lamp, Clyde H. 58
Landis, Aaron 96
Landis, Alice Maud 47
Landis, Amanda G. Keller 58
Landis, Amos Stauffer 47
Landis, Anna E. 58
Landis, Austin E. 47
Landis, Bessie Anna 47
Landis, Brenda 93
Landis, Chester 58
Landis, Clayton 58
Landis, Elwood E.47
Landis, Enos Clayton 47
Landis, Esther Naomi 47
Landis, Fanny 45
Landis, Florence Sabina 48
Landis, Frank 58
Landis, Franklin 27
Landis, Grace E. 58
Landis, Henry 20
Landis, Herman 74
Landis, Jacob 20
Landis, John 7
landis, john E.. 58
Landis, John Frick 58
Landis, Katie E. 58
Landis, Lena May 47
Landis, Mabel E. 58
Landis, Mary E. 58
Landis, Mary Frances 47
Landis, MennoClaude 47
Landis, Michael Wanner 96
landis, Paris E. 58
Landis, Paul E. 58
Landis, Ruth E. 59
Landis, Ruth Wio 48
Landis, Vesta 96
Landis, Walter E. 58

Lefever, Mary A. 40
Lehman, Anna R. 28
Lehman, Barbara 20
Lehman, Esther Burkholder 6
Lehman, Peter 28
Lehman, Susan 20
Light, Barbara 13
Light, Elizabeth 14
Light, Henry 14
Light, Jacob 14
Logan, Charles D.- 26
Long, Ruth C. 50
Longenecker, Abraham 20
Longenecker, Amanda 20
Longenkcker, Annie 20
Longenecker, Beatrice wilhelm 101
Longenecker, Christian 18, 20
Longenecker, David 20
Longenecker, Elizabeth Lehman 72
Longenecker, Esther 20
Longenecker, Fannie 20
Longenecker, Fanny B. 18
Longenecker, Fanny Brenneman 20
Longenecker, George 34
Longenecker, Henry E. 20
Longenecker, Henry R. 20
Longenecker, John 20
Longenecker, Lizzie 20
Longenecker, Magdalena Hollinger 34
Longenecker, Robert N. 101
Longenecker, Ruth Ann 101
Longenecker, Samuek E. 20,72
Longenecker, Susan S. Lehman 72
Longenecker, Veronica Brenneman 18
Louser, Herman 102
Louser, Mabel Roush 102

Louser, Ruth Louise 102
Martin, Addison 43
Martin, Anna 22
Martin, Harvey Hoffer 58
Maulfair, Clara Alice 67
Maulfair, Elijah 67
Maulfair, Loouisa 67
McCord, Joh 14
Meck, Donald 91
Mellinger, Benedict 2
Mellinger, Christian 3
Mellinger, Mary Hershey 2
Mellinger, Veronica 2, 13
Meyer, Henry L. 23
Miller, Alice E. 58
Miller, Anna E. 60
Miller, David F. 100
Miller, Esther B. 78
Miller, Jesse 100
Miller, J. Herbert 100
Miller, John H. 100
Miller, Louise rinehart 100
Mohler, Ralph E. 95
Miller, Robert C. 100
Mohn, Elizabeth Killian Beheney 93
Mohn, Lorraine L. 93
Mohn, Roy 93
Molesevich, 104
Moonshine, George 92
Moonshine, John A. 92
Moonshine, John Leroy 92
Moonshine, Sallie 92
Moonshine, Sherman Daniel 92
Moonshine, Sherri Lynn 93
Moose, Cztharinie 90
Moyer, Elizabeth 5
Moyer, Frany 33
Moyer, John 13

Moyer, Martin 33, 42
Moyer, Mary 17
Moyer, Mary Kreider 33
Mulll, Jim 82
Mumma, AnnaE. 45
Mumma, Christian 45
Mumma, Martin 45
Mumma, Martin L. 45
Mumma, Mary E. 45
Mumma, Michael 42
Mumma, Nancy Nissley 45
Musser, Anna 73
Musser, Enos S. 73
Musser, Howard M. 73
Mutch, Minerva Elizabeth 67
Mutch, Henry 67
Mutch, Sallie 67
Myers, Bernice 85
Myers, Mary D. 23
Naftzger, Adam 37
Naftzger, Carrie 37
Naftzger, Clayton 37
Naftzger, Elizabeth 37
Naftzger, John A. 37
Naftzger, Joseph 37
Nagle, Clarence 104
Newcomer, Adam 40
Nice, Ruth 49
Nickel, Harry M. 42
Nickel, Earl Wayne 42
Nickel, Emma May 42
Nissley, Anna 24
Nissley, Gertrude 6, 12
Nissley, John 6, 24
Nissley, Joseph 78
Nissley, PaulE. 78

Ober, Elmer M. 97

Ober, John 60
Ober, Minnie Oberholtzer 97
Ober, Ruth Marie 97
Ober, Sara 60
Oldweiler, Albert 56
Oldweiler, Amanda 56
Oldweiler, Clayton 56
Oldweiler, Cyrus 56
Oldweiler, Harry 56
Oldweiler, Isaiah 56
Oldweiler, Oliver 56
Oldweiler, William 56
Over, Addie 27
Parmer, John D. 26
Peiffer, Harold H. G. 70
Peiffer, Howard 70
Prestin, Homas J. 68
Preston, Ila Ruth 67
Preston, Urada Walker 68
Reisner, John Leonard 47
Reisner, Anna Catharine 47
Reisner, Lewis A. 47
Reisner, Mary Ellen 47
Reisner, Naomi Esther 47
Reisner, Charles Leonard 47
Rethfon, Esther, Pear Ferguson 92
Rethfon, Leigh 92
Rethfon, Robert Lee 92
Rhoads, Earl w. 53
Rhoads, H. S. 53
Rhoads, Lloyd 53
Rhodes, Anna Martin 61
Rhodes, John 61
Rhodes, Nancy 61
Rice, Ray G. 55
Richi, Roger 92
Ricker, Arthur E. 71
Ricker, Blanche M. 71

Ricker, Claude 71
Ricker, Elizabeth 71
Ricker, Henry 71
Ricker, J.Henry 71
Ricker, Mary e. 71
Ricker, Ralph A. 71
Ricker, Ulysses 71
Riegel, Martha 73
Rignati, John 103
Rignati, Rita Grillo103
Rignati, Rocco 103
Risser, Abraham 44
Risser, Amanda 44
Risser, Elizabeth 63
Risser, Ellen 44
Risser. Ephraim 23
Risser, Fannie Nissley 43
Risser, Joseph 43
Risser, Lillian H. 77
Risser, Luella 97
Risser, Mary 9
Risser, Mary N. 43
Ritzman, Arthur 44
Root, Mary 40
Rutt, Abraham 42, 43
Rutt, Anna Ebersole 19
Rutt, Annie 26
Rutt, Barbara 3, 42
Rutt, Christian 3
Rutt, Edwin 42
Rutt, Fannie 42
Rutt, Ellen 42
Rutt, Peter 3
Rutt, Samuel 26
Rutt, Susanna 26
Rutter, Elizabeth M. 54
Rutter, Zamuel S. 54
Sandoe, Elizabeth Stibgeen 63

Sandoe, Henry 63
Sandoe, Mary 63
Sauder, Amos 94
Sauder, Anna JHoover 94
Sauder, Elizabeth 94
Saylor, Mabel 78
Schreffler, Randall 106
Sellers, Abner E. 70
Sellers, Abner P. 90
Sellers, Pearl S.70, 89
Sellers, Rhoda K. 70, 90
Sellers, Susan p. 90
Shanaman, Fannie Knoll 66
Shanaman, Frany Knoll 66
Shanaman, Samuel 66
Shank, Frances E. 78
Shank, Norman H. 60
Shearer, ChristianL. 88
Shearer, Laura Laber 88
Shearer, Ruth 88
Shenk, Benjamin 24
Shenk, Estelle 74
Shenk, Jacob G. 74
Shenk, Jacob K. 35
Shenk, John 74
Shenk, Mary 74
shenk, Walter 744
Shenk, Minerva E. 35
Shenk, Sarah 12
Sholly, Connie Ann 92
Sholly, Harold 92
Sholly Sandra 92
Shuman, Li 42
Shuman, Elizabeth Mann 42
Shuman, Margaret 42
Shuey, Anna Elizabeth 82
Shuey, Calvin Hrrison 82
Shuey, David Calvin 82

Shuey, Edward 82
Shuey, Jacob Edward 82
Shuey, Rosanna Boyer 82
Shuey, Viola May 82
Sims, Jared 100
Sims, John 100
Skinner, James 71
Smith, Joseph L. 56
Smith, Pamela Susan 104
Snavely, Edward M. 45
Snavely, Phares 50
Snoke, Sallie 66
Snyder, John 44
Sonders, Sarah 10
Speraw, Dorothy 103
Starr, Richard Adair 97
Stauffer, Anna Mae 73
Stauffer, Barbara Buckwalter 45
Stober, Cathariine Miller 90
Stober, Earl 91
Stober, Grace 91
Stober, Joseph P. 90
Stober, Martin 91
Stohler, Mary A. 102
Stover, Paul V. 90
Stover, Christian 2
Soulliard, W, R. 50
Sucec, Frank 91
Tice, John 104
Tice, Mary Showers 104
Tice, William Patrick 104
Tennis, Anna Marie 92
Tennis, Carol Ann 92
Tennis, Christian Ebersole 80
Tennis, Donald Lee 92
Tennis, Elvin L. 91
Tennus, Fannie Fackler 79
Tennis, Jacob 91

Tennis, Jacob Samuel, 80
Tennis, Joseph Irvin 80
Tennis, Katie Dorcas 80
Tennis, Larry G.91
Tennis, Mary Elizabeth 80, 92
Tennis, Mervin J. 91
Tennis, Miriam Esther 91
Tennis, Nelson Ray 92
Tennis, Samuel 91
Tennis, Samuel S. 79
Thummel, Bertha Powers 48
Troutman, Edith Groff 102
Troutman, Henry 102
Troutman, William Henry 102
Wagner, Judith Ann 103
Walker, Anita Rebecca 97
Walker, Charles Francis 96, 97
Walker, Ira 97
Walker, Nancy Marie 97
Walker, Stanley Kenneth 97
Walker, Rebecca Dundore 97
Walmer, Carrie Frantz, 104
Walmer, David M. 103
Walmer, Diane Louise 103
Walmer, Marvin M.103
Wampler, Delphie Hale 85
Wampler, Effie V. 85
Wampler, Homer 85
Wampler, richard C. 85
Weaber, Frank H. 60
Weaver, Adaline 12
Weaver, E. S. 60
Weaver, Harvey T. 60
Weaver, Mary 2
Weber, Annie - 3
Weber, John - 3
Weidner, Ellen 58
Weikert, L.Bertha 88

Weir, Solomon 5
Wert,Joseph E. 58
Westenberger, David 64
Westenberger, Sarah C. 64
Westenberger, Sarah Gossert 64
Wheeler, Weldon 42
Whisler, Benjammin 77
Whisler, Clara 76
White, EllaStoohler 100
White, Harry L.100
White, Heidi Ann 100
White, Horace P. 100
White, Richard Allen 99
Wine, George E.98
Wine, Hazel Heatwole 98
Wine, June Caroline 98
Winters, Abram 61
Winters, Louise Alwine 61
Winters, ruth A. 61
Witmer, Adam32
Witmer, Anna 24
Witmer, Barbar Lehman 13
Witmer, Emma 33
Witmer, Franklin 33
witmer, Jacob 6, 13
Witmer, John A. 33
Witmeyer, Cyrus B. 66
Witmeyer, John A. 66
Wittle, Christian 60
Wolfe, David 83
Wolfe, Ella M. 83
Wolfe, rosanna Rutter 83
Yeaglerry, Priscilla 33
Young, Mary 60
Zeager, Mary A. 30
Zeager, Paul 58
Zehring, Josephine Janet 99
Zehring, William H. 99

www.ingramcontent.com/pod-product-compliance
Lightning Source LLC
Chambersburg PA
CBHW080335270326
41927CB00014B/3236